The Authorities

Powerful Wisdom from Leaders in the Field

KIRK JAKESTA

Award Winning Author

AuthoritiesPress

Copyright © 2019, 2021 Authorities Press

ISBN: 978-1-77277-309-5

Limits of Liability and Disclaimer of Warranty
The author and publisher shall not be liable for your misuse of the enclosed material. This book is strictly for informational and educational purposes.

Warning – Disclaimer
The purpose of this book is to educate and entertain. The author and/or publisher do not guarantee that anyone following these techniques, suggestions, tips, ideas, or strategies will become successful. The author and/or publisher shall have neither liability nor responsibility to anyone with respect to any loss or damage caused, or alleged to be caused, directly or indirectly by the information contained in this book.

Medical Disclaimer
The medical or health information in this book is provided as an information resource only, and is not to be used or relied on for any diagnostic or treatment purposes. This information is not intended to be patient education, does not create any patient-physician relationship, and should not be used as a substitute for professional diagnosis and treatment.

Publisher
Authorities Press
Markham, ON
Canada

Printed in the United States and Canada.

FOREWORD

Experts are to be admired for their knowledge, but they often remain unrecognized by the general public because they save their information and insights for paying customers and clients. There are many experts in a given field, but their impact is limited to the handful of people with whom they work.

Unlike experts, authorities share their knowledge and expertise far more broadly, so they make a big impact on the world. Authorities become known and admired as leading experts and, as such, typically do very well economically and professionally. Most authorities are also mature enough to know that part of the joy of monetary success is the accompanying moral and spiritual obligation to give back.

Many people want to learn and work with well-respected and generous authorities, but don't always know where to find them. They may be known to their peers, or within a specific community, but have not had the opportunity to reach a wider audience. At one time, they might have submitted a proposal to the *For Dummies* or *Chicken Soup for the Soul* series of books, but it's now almost impossible to get accepted as a new author in such a branded book series.

It is more than fitting that Raymond Aaron, an internationally known and respected authority in his own right, would be the one to recognize the need for a new venue in which authorities could share their considerable knowledge with readers everywhere. As the only author ever to be included in both of the book series mentioned above, Raymond has had the opportunity to give back and he understands how crucial it is for authorities to have a platform from which to share their expertise.

I have known and worked with Raymond for a number of years and consider him a valued friend and talented coach. He knows how to spot talented and knowledgeable people and he desires to see them prosper. Over the years, success coaching and speaking engagements around the world have made it possible for Raymond to meet many of these talented authorities. He recognizes and relates to their passion and enthusiasm for what they do, as well as their desire to share what they know. He tells me that's why he has created this new nonfiction branded book series, *The Authorities.*

Dr. Nido Qubein
President, High Point University

TABLE OF CONTENTS

INTRODUCTION

This book introduces you to *The Authorities* — individuals who have distinguished themselves in life and in business. Authorities make a big impact on the world. Authorities are leaders in their chosen fields. Authorities typically do very well financially, and are evolved enough to know that part of the joy of monetary success is the accompanying social, moral and spiritual obligation to give back.

Authorities are not just outstanding. They are also *known* to be outstanding.

This additional element begins to explain the difference between two strategic business and life concepts — one that seems great, but isn't, and the other that fills in the essential missing gap of the first.

The first concept is "the expert."

What is an expert? The real definition is ...

EXPERT: *a person who knows stuff*

People who have attained a very senior academic degree (like a PhD or an MD) definitely know stuff. People who read voraciously and retain what they read definitely know stuff. Unfortunately, just because you know stuff does not mean that anyone respects the fact that you do. Even though some experts are successful, alas, most are not — because knowing stuff is not enough.

Well, then, what is the missing piece?

What the expert lacks, "the authority" has. The authority both knows stuff and is *known* to know stuff. So, more simply ...

AUTHORITY: *a person who is known as an expert*

The difference is not subtle. The difference is not merely semantic. The difference is enormous.

When it comes to this subject, there are actually three categories in which people fall:

- People who don't know much and are unsuccessful in life and in business. Most people fall in this category.

- People who know stuff, but still don't leave much of a footprint in the world. There are a lot of people like this.

- Experts who are also *known* as experts become authorities and authorities are always wondrously successful. Authorities are able to contribute more to humanity through both their chosen work and their giving back.

This book is about the highest category, *The Authorities* — people who have reached the peak in their field and are known as such.

You will definitely know some of *The Authorities* in this book, especially since there are some world-famous ones. Others are just as exceptional, but you may not yet know about them. Let me introduce you to Kirk Jakesta, our featured author.

Our circumstances can create challenges in our lives, ones that can feel impossible to overcome, at least not without a major change to our mindset. In *Break Down the Box: Taking a Risk to Create an Amazing Life*, Kirk Jakesta shares his journey on how to change your mindset and learn to take risks. One of the first and most critical aspects of Kirk's journey was learning how to change his mindset. Throughout his chapter, you can learn how to change your mindset, as well as how doing so can impact your life in a positive way.

Kirk also shares his goal of being a role model to members of the First

Nations, who may have been dealt challenging circumstances. Along the way, he shares how his mentors have inspired him to take risks and open the door to opportunities. Then he focuses on the importance of finding inspiration and mentors to motivate you to keep moving forward.

From the beginning of *Break Down the Box*, Kirk starts challenging the excuses you might use to keep from creating change in your life. He reminds you how critical it is to create your own happiness, not tying it to the actions of others or circumstances that life presents you.

Additionally, Kirk shares the tools that inspired him to create a new life for himself, and how you can use them to your benefit. He shares how you can refocus your mind by taking the time to be quiet, and focus on your dreams and goals. Life can be draining, distracting you from achieving all that is possible in your life. Instead of making do with what you have, it is key to change your mindset and avoid mental quicksand.

If you are ready to make a big change, then enjoy *Break Down the Box*. Start the process of changing your mindset, and learn to take risks, in order to change your life!

They are *The Authorities*. Learn from them. Connect with them. Let them uplift you. Learning from them and working with them is the secret ingredient for success which may well allow you to rise to the level of Authority soon.

To be considered for inclusion in a subsequent edition of *The Authorities*, register to attend a future event at www.aaron.com/events where you will be interviewed and considered.

Break Down the Box

Taking a Risk to Create an Amazing Life

KIRK JAKESTA

Become who you were meant to be.

Listen to that voice in the back of your head that says, "I could do this."

Growing up as a young man, I quickly adapted to the lifestyle that was presented to me, a life that threatened to consume me, sending me into the dark path of life, if I were to let it. Where the thought of change seemed out of reach.

Perhaps you grew up in a lifestyle like mine where drug and alcohol abuse were the norm, where selling drugs as a young adolescent wasn't unusual but accepted, or you grew up in a good wholesome environment where life just made you comfortable with what you had. Deep down, we always want more. We want the best that life has to offer. In the back of our mind, our thoughts tell us that we are not worthy of it. We deal with the hand life dealt us and face the tough financial challenges without a leg to stand on, believing that we are not worthy of better.

Just getting by was my specialty, and still is. It was my normal growing up. My father who is now in his mid late 70's, worked his ass off for a better part of 60 years of his life in order to provide. Working construction camp jobs, spending half a year and sometimes more away from home to be able to provide a comfortable living for my family and I. Now, even though there isn't anything to retire on comfortably he has finally come to terms with retirement due to his health limitations that come with his age.

My mother, who is one of my best friends, is in her late 50's now and she suffers from Osteoporosis and for me that's a hard pill to swallow. Seeing your parents' health deteriorate, especially after growing up thinking that we will all live forever. My parents have been the best, they gave me a good life. Despite growing up the way I did, my parents have been my crutch, and shaped me into the man I am today. Teaching me what's right from wrong, teaching me to be a gentleman, a provider, a man that can achieve great things. Along with the influence of my brothers and grandparents and other family members throughout my life, I want to be someone great, for them.

We all have close friends and family, whose aging has brought the reality of losing them closer to mind. Many of us have lost close family and friends to sudden loss. As life goes on, it's clear that we are all living off of borrowed time, tomorrow is never promised, and the best time to create a life worth living is NOW. My loved ones inspired me, and I want to inspire those who need it. To show that no matter where you are in life, there is always a fork in the road. If you are brave enough to look past the fear of starting something new, then you will realize that life's greatest experiences are usually on the other side of fear. I want you to recognize that you deserve to tap into the greatness inside you! There is more to life that we are missing out on.

Previous years have brought some amazing opportunities my way, but first, I had to let go of my fixed mindset and adapt a growth mindset. I had to take action and show up to reap the benefits. I'll admit, it took a major shift in my thinking, and it's a constant battle against procrastination, self-doubt and fear of failure. Even as I write this chapter, I realize that it took a lot to get to this point. I had to crawl out of that hole of self-pity, dust myself off and get back into the game. I needed to step beyond what I saw as possible in my everyday life, and instead believe that I had what it takes to propel me forward, only if I was willing to take that leap of faith to create significant change.

Starting with my first self-development program, a seed was planted in me. I gained the mindset to be my own boss one day. To stop working 8-12 hours a day on another man's dream. When we think about how much free time we have, how much of it is wasted? Think about it; the average person sleeps 8 hours a day and works for 8 hours a day. That's 16 hours dedicated to sustaining a living and getting the proper sleep. There are 8 remaining hours that most of us aren't taking full advantage of. I know there are other essential activities that are accounted for in those 8 remaining hours, but you get the gist of it. I came to recognize that I could make my life extraordinary, but I NEEDED TO CHANGE MY MINDSET to tap into my ability. One of the hardest people you will ever have to battle is yourself.

Imagine stepping out on faith like that in your life. Having a vision for your future and then taking a leap without the proverbial safety net. My leap led me to many mentors and opportunities. Opportunities like becoming an award-winning author by taking the leap and jumping into a book deal with an amazing powerhouse, world renowned speakers, authors, entrepreneurs, and now my co-authors, with the goal to pursue a speaking career to inspire First Nations people around the world and starting my own digital marketing agency to serve small to medium sized businesses and help them survive during a pandemic. Note that all those opportunities gave back to me in a big way. They helped me to mentally prepare for the next opportunity, the next open door, and the next chapter in my journey towards an amazing life.

Each step I took led me to another networking opportunity, another inspiration, another mentor, and the momentum continues to build. I put myself on the path to find those "once in a lifetime" opportunities. Now I want to reach out to my people, becoming a role model and demonstrating that all things are possible. There is a life outside of your conditions, which is the reverse of the way you are living. It is possible to create a brighter future, but it starts with believing in yourself. Dedicate yourself to something, then great things will happen. You do not have to be a victim of your circumstances. Instead, you can take charge and be the change in your life.

You do not have to remain affected by our grandparents and parents unfortunate past of residential school, and the horrible ripple effect of what they went through. For those who don't understand what they went through, that ripple effect has affected us all through the generations in one way or the other. Now is the time to stop that ripple effect by making conscious choices in our lives to create change.

We must take responsibility for our past choices and actions, but more importantly, the ones we are making in the present. The present is all you can change, but the possibilities are endless if you are willing to move through the fear of the unknown and the fear of failure.

The point I want to make throughout this chapter is that you have the power to create, to build, and to change. It all starts with a willingness to open your mind to the possibilities and even to take risks to achieve what you have always dreamed of, even if you may have denied your ability to create that vision in the past.

I am here to tell you that all things are possible. You do not have to struggle through an endless loop of paychecks, overwhelming debt, and the hardship of not having the necessities. You do not have to let a troubled past get in the way of your amazing future. Instead, you can have a life that is rich in personal meaning and leaves a legacy behind for your children and grandchildren.

CULTURE IS THE FOUNDATION FOR GROWTH

Our culture is one based on close-knit families and time-honored traditions. For hundreds of years, we lived in harmony with the land and each other. Time has changed things, and modern life does not seem to focus on this rich cultural heritage. I even find that the way I was raised limited my access to my culture, disconnecting me from what should be a greater part of my life, although I believe strongly that it is never too late to learn and make it a part of my family's life. I will continue to put forth the effort to make that happen even if it's with only little snippets throughout our lives.

What cultural heritage am I referring to? I am First Nations. I represent Nisga'a Nation, from the village of Gitlaxt'aamiks or New Aiyansh, and from my father's side. I am part of the Tahltan Nation. These are parts of who I am, although I truly wish the connection with these cultures was an even stronger part of my daily life. Still, it doesn't stop me from being who I am.

Why isn't it a greater part of my life? My childhood was not easy. I would say that I was undereducated, as the school system in my village was rated the second lowest in British Columbia. On top of that, we had a house built in the early 2000's. A few years after we moved in, we had a kitchen fire. It did a lot of smoke damage to the kitchen, leaving it completely charred. Nothing was done to fix it. That is a mindset that I grew up with, one where you learned to live with what you had. There wasn't an expectation that we deserved to have the kitchen fixed and, 15 years after the fire, that damage is still there. This is the reality of where I came from and who I am. So, you can see why I would want more out of life.

What about your own life? Can you see places where damage was done, but you did nothing to fix it? All of us deal with some type of psychological, physical, or emotional trauma. It could be a result of choices we made, or the actions of others that were not in our control. This world is a cruel place. In the end, however, it is up to you to decide if you want to live as a victim or be a victor instead.

Growing up with my two older brothers, I was confronted with circumstances that I could have blamed for my life choices. At home, there was a lot of fighting, drinking, and smoking weed. It was a tough environment for a young adolescent but that was my normal. Around 15 or 16 years old, I went from being a recreational marijuana smoker to dealing the herb. In fact, I became one of the biggest weed dealers in the community at one point. Then I moved to hustling harder drugs, to the point where I was making good money for a teenager. I didn't feel that great about myself or what I was doing to get that money. However, the lifestyle was so different from the years that my family struggled that it was hard to turn my back on the money.

That all changed the day that one of my friends offered herself to me as payment for drugs. It felt like an incredibly low point in my life. I started asking myself what I was doing. This was not who I was meant to be. I was completely shocked by her offer, and I couldn't accept it. I ended up giving her the drugs for nothing and quitting that business. I was done contributing to tearing down myself and others. Now I had to figure out how I was going to build myself back up and, in the process, how I could help others do the same. The answers were still a few years away, but I was at least on the track to finding them.

If I had not stopped then, I could have ended up in jail, dead, or with the death of someone else on my conscience. Your choices create your future. By making the choice to get out of that life, I changed my own future and I am grateful for it. I learned at a young age that life is truly about moments. Moments where you can either take the road less travelled or the same one as everyone else. Even though I didn't acknowledge it back then, I was making these life-changing decisions. I can see now that my conscience was in the right place.

That rough environment offered few opportunities for young people like me. As I got out of the drug world, I realized that I couldn't stay where I was. I needed to create an opportunity for myself. So, I headed to Vancouver, where I attended Vancouver Island University Trade School. I took classes to be an automotive service technician. After graduating, it became clear that this wasn't the future for me either. The men in the trade hated their jobs, and I realized I didn't want to be one of them. I was at peace with that. Even though I dedicated almost a year of my life to achieve that certification, I knew deep down I couldn't sacrifice my life to unfulfillment and regret.

I felt as if I was going through the process of elimination. The knowledge about what didn't work for me was as valuable as the knowledge about what did work for me. I started to understand myself better and believe that my happiness was mine to create.

CREATING HAPPINESS STARTS WITH YOU

Happiness is not going to magically appear because of the things you own or the fact that you work 60 to 80 hours a week to bring home a paycheck. Instead, happiness is a state of mind, one that you can create, no matter your circumstances.

My determination to create change in my life led me to leave behind a life of drug dealing, and countless dead-end jobs. For almost a decade, I have lived in Vancouver, where I started to do all kinds of different work, exploring my interests and trying to find my place in this world. I learned a lot about what I was good at, what I was okay at, and what I just struggled to accomplish.

During this time of exploration, I was still a typical young man, out to meet girls, party and live life for the weekends. Not the most ideal lifestyle, but it was the life of a young man with few responsibilities. Then my daughter was born. She is my biggest inspiration, and I knew that I wanted to give her a better life than the one I had. Now I was inspired to do better, even if I wasn't sure how. I believed that if I did almost everything in the opposite way I was raised, I was going to be fine. In order to do that, I needed a new set of skills, and I needed a new way of thinking about the world and my place in it.

It was about becoming the role model that I wish I had when I was growing up, and finding inspiration in the young girl that now depended on me. To give her happiness, I had to be willing to claim it for myself to be able to provide a better life for her and my entire family. I'm a strong believer in "When I make it, we all make it."

Your happiness is a state of mind. You are in charge of your mind, not your circumstances. You can choose what to dwell on, and your point of view. I want to challenge you to recognize that you need to change your mindset about the circumstances themselves, thus creating happiness for yourself no matter where life currently has planted you.

IS NEGATIVE THINKING HOLDING YOU BACK?

Some individuals seem to naturally be able to find the silver lining of any situation, and their joy in life is apparent. Even when they are faced with difficult circumstances, they focus on what they can learn and how they can grow, instead of becoming defeated. Granted, that does not come naturally to everyone. In fact, many of us are quick to fall into a negative way of thinking, one that keeps us focused on what has gone wrong and keeps us from acting decisively.

The reason I point this out is because if you want to achieve real change in your life, you need to be able to act decisively. A negative mindset will keep you from acting, simply because you will spend all your time talking yourself out of doing anything. The excuses can be numerous. Here are just a few:

- I don't have the money.

- I don't have the education.

- I don't have the skills.

- Those adventures are for other people. I have a family to take care of.

- The risk is just too great.

Negative thinking means that you tend to value the risk higher than the reward, so you freeze yourself in place, living with circumstances that you aren't excited about, simply because you can't accept the potential of risk.

Now if you aren't able to accept risk and you have a negative frame of mind, it can be very difficult to create the happiness you seek in your own life. It must start with a change to your own mindset, one that acknowledges risks but is not defined or held down by them. At the same time, I am not talking about a pie-in-the-sky type of thinking, the kind that cannot recognize challenges or potential issues.

Risk assessment is still a part of life, but the focus needs to be on how to mitigate the risk, not how to avoid acting so that you can avoid the risk altogether. When your mindset is in a positive frame, you are going to find that you look at risk differently. It is not an impasse or an obstacle that stops you from moving forward. Instead, you view it as something to be addressed, a challenge that can be navigated effectively. For every problem in life, there is a solution. The only thing that stops us is fear itself.

When you are focused on just surviving, and not on thriving, then no matter what soil you are planted in or the circumstances that you find yourself in, you are never going to be truly happy. In the quest for small moments of happiness, you are likely to make choices that are going to negatively impact yourself and those that you love.

Those choices could be anything, from bad investments, addictions, toxic relationships. The point is that, long term, those choices are going to negatively impact your ability to make your situation better. Instead, you have now made your road even harder. Now you have another set of challenges to deal with, and those additional difficulties can be truly crushing to your mind and spirit.

Can you relate to some of these choices or ways of thinking? Can you understand negative thinking and using words like "can't," "won't," or "shouldn't" are keeping you from achieving what you were put on this earth to accomplish? As you can see, negative thinking can break down your spirit and leave you feeling as if you don't have the strength or ability to create change in your life. It can leave you feeling that your life is what it is, and you are better off just to accept it. I'm here to say f#!k that. Go Get Yours!

You are never truly stuck unless you choose to be. Can you find some light in the darkness, that inspiration and motivation you need to take the first step? I found it in my daughter, but it was also clear that I was changing my thinking and that was impacting my future in ways that I couldn't yet imagine.

MANIFESTING YOUR NEW REALITY STARTS WITH YOU

During the time before my daughter was born, I had that moment all new fathers do, questioning the finances and trying to figure out how to provide for this new miracle in my life.

My answer was civil construction, which led me to eventually becoming a heavy equipment operator. I picked up the experience needed by jumping into a piece of equipment every chance I got. Straight up, I manifested that into reality. I had it in my mind when I first stepped foot in the field as a laborer, watching the guys run those big machines, that one day "that would be me."

Are there areas in your life where you need to be aggressive to achieve a goal? I could have sat back and waited for someone to give me an opportunity to learn how to operate those machines, but the truth is, that day might never have come. By seizing the reins, I created the opportunities for myself and achieved my goal. It wasn't easy, and I had to make some sacrifices. For two years, I worked the night shift. Starting out as the lowest paid laborer (which was still good money for a new soon-to-be father) and working myself up to be a lead hand. Delegating tasks and executing them in a safe timely matter. Here is where my life revolved around eating, sleeping, and going to work. I couldn't do anything else, and it wasn't the healthiest lifestyle. But it was also the first time that I manifested one of my goals, and it wasn't going to be my last.

In spite of all that negative thinking from my past, I decided to take a leap beyond what I had already accomplished. I decided that I didn't have to work to barely make ends meet for the rest of my life. I did have the ability to leave something for my daughter, and I had the power to create a legacy, one that would impact the generations to follow. The question was how?

START WITH INSPIRATION AND ADD ACTION

No matter who you are and where you are in your life, there are individuals who inspire you. They are the ones who accomplish so much, despite the challenges and those who tell them that it can't be done. Yes, there are plenty of people out there who are going to tell you that nothing can change, you are risking too much, and that you will be sorry later. They might even claim that they are telling you these things for your own good, so that they can protect you.

That is not the kind of protection that you need. Instead, you need to be willing to take the risk, even be willing to fail. Fail forward. After all, if you never fail, then you will never know what it takes to succeed. You need to step beyond the opinions of others, beyond the fear, to have more, be more, and experience more.

To put it simply, failure is just a way of eliminating a process that wasn't going to work, thus allowing you to focus your time and energy on other options that might be more successful. At this point it is not a secret anymore.

It's out in the open and has been for decades; failure is the crucial ingredient for success. You must treat each failure as part of the elimination process, one more step closer to achieving your goal. Eventually, something will give, and you will get the right idea or find the solution to your problem. This is a guaranteed result of dedicating your thoughts to your goal, and you best believe it works to the opposite effect as well. Your thoughts navigate your life. Whichever road you choose to go down is directly controlled by your own thoughts.

My goal was to achieve a better life for my family, and that meant figuring out what I was good at and what I wasn't good at. Simply choosing to abandon a course of action that isn't working can feel so liberating. Plus, every time you remove yourself from a course of action that isn't working, you are moving yourself closer to achieving your goals!

The inspiration for my next course change came as I realized that my mind was not fully in my work. I operate heavy machinery, which is not a job where you can afford to be distracted.

Instead, you need to stay focused on what you are doing and keeping the people around you safe as you complete the task at hand. Once I realized that I was in the place where I couldn't keep that level of focus, I knew I needed to take a break. It was my moment to take a leap and see where it would lead. I was inspired by several individuals, ones who took risks and were willing to give everything to make big changes in their lives.

Even though at the time, after a bit of a hiatus, the skills that I picked up after all those years have given me the credibility to take on a supervisor roll after only two months coming back to the same line of work. That is a testament to the dedication that I once had to this specific line of work. Even though I knew this wouldn't be for the rest of my life, it feels good to know that I have what it takes to walk on to a new job, take control, and quickly establish myself in a key role.

What are you willing to give up? I bet you might be thinking that you aren't willing to give up much. Your life is comfortable, you have a routine, and even if it isn't everything that you hoped it would be, at least you understand the rules and expectations. That is where we all get tripped up from time to time. We choose the devil we know versus the devil we don't, because the unknown is scary. It is a dark hole and we don't know what might be hiding in there or lurking just around the corner. The truth is that what is lurking around the corner could be amazing, but too many times, we miss those opportunities because we are afraid to look.

Part of changing your mindset means accepting that taking leaps is critical to your success. The unknown is a place that allows you to grow and really craft your vision for your life. Fear is what keeps us in one place, holding onto things that might not benefit us, but are comforting because of their familiarity.

Think about it this way. If you know how to achieve a result using one process, you are likely to continue to use that process. However, if that process doesn't work as well as you like, you might explore other options and open yourself up to the idea of trying something different.

While that might work in the processes you complete at work, when it comes to taking greater risks in your professional and personal lives, there is a tendency to do the opposite. We tend to focus on dealing with the broken process, instead of trying to find an alternative and exploring other opportunities.

On the other hand, when I opened my mind up to the possibilities, I also unlocked my potential to create the life I had envisioned for myself. Therefore, be willing to be open to the possibilities. Do not lock yourself into one way of thinking, thus creating tunnel vision regarding what you are capable of accomplishing.

Even if the way that you are doing things has been successful in the past, you need to remember that life is not black and white. There is more than one way to skin a deer. What works successfully for one individual might not work as well for you. Don't be quick to lock yourself into one way of doing things, and thus be unwilling to consider other options.

Our world and society are geared to locking you into a position or a way of thinking, and then discourage you from taking the chance to make a change. Yet, those who have been the most successful, the ones who have created real shifts in how our world functions, started out by taking risks, breaking out of the expectations that had been put on them.

It is adapting a growth mindset and never accepting defeat that helped me to start a business in Digital Marketing as well as becoming a published author and one day a speaker that will inspire countless Indigenous people around the world. You can create that type of change in your life too! You just have to be willing to stop worrying about what people will think of you. Succeed or not, it's your life. Do what's best for YOU.

It involves breaking out of the box, taking a risk, and then reaping the rewards from stepping onto the path less traveled.

UNDERSTANDING THE EXPECTATIONS THAT KEEP YOU LOCKED IN

A part of any society is the fact that expectations are built into how we are shaped. Cultures include specific events to mark our passage into adulthood.

From our courtships through the building of our families, certain expectations are put into place for all of us, based on where we grow up and how we are raised. What can happen, however, is that those expectations can end up being roadblocks that keep us from moving forward and tapping our full potential.

In my childhood, there were multiple roadblocks; circumstances that could have kept me stuck on a path that left me feeling unfulfilled and unable to care for my daughter in a way that I wanted to. I could have continued the cycle of drug dealing and dysfunction, but I decided to go out into the unknown. You have the power to do the same!

Therefore, I want you to think about the expectations that are part of your life. Are they serving you now or are they blocking you from moving forward? The biggest problem for some of my people is that the expectations are often set too low and our resources are often limited, and we are left with the acceptance that we have reached our full potential.

However, I know that there is more out there for all of us. It starts with a willingness to act on our own behalf, not waiting for someone else to do it for us. We must lose that sense of entitlement because nobody owes us anything. It's up to us to put forth the work that is needed to achieve what we want in life.

Every belief and value you have contributes to the decisions you make, and how you choose to act. Those beliefs and values can be altered as you experience different events throughout your life. Now you can choose to take those experiences and allow them to help you sift through those values and beliefs.

Do you regularly take the time to examine your values and beliefs? Do you ever ask yourself why you believe what you do, or why you value one thing over another? The reason it is important to do so is because you are going to make automatic decisions that impact your future based on those beliefs and values. Shouldn't they reflect who you are now instead of who you used to be?

Recognize that, whether you want to or not, you are constantly being exposed to influences that are changing and shaping you. How are you responding to this shaping? Many of us don't even consciously recognize how we are being altered by these forces, but once you are conscious of how these influences are impacting you, you can choose to accept or reject them. Take this for an example: McDonalds has their advertising everywhere. Literally globally. Everywhere you look, whether it's a billboard, on social media or television. Advertising for their new promotional meal or drink is constantly being programmed into your brain, so when you are hungry or thirsty you subconsciously have the thought of the new stuff instantly pop up in your head. This is all brainwash. The same goes for anything you allow into your brain, even a daily dose of inspiration. So be cautious of what you allow in and choose wisely.

Part of the importance of recognizing these influences is that many of them can keep you in a state of denial about the possibilities in your life. Others could be trying to keep you safe, so they discourage you from taking what they believe to be unnecessary chances. Still others are just negative in general and will tend to bring up everything that could go wrong, every potential obstacle, and even attack your intelligence for thinking about giving it a try.

Notice that those influencers in your circle are fundamentally trying to block you from taking a path that they may have decided not to walk themselves. They truly believe that if a course of action wasn't a fit for them, then it is not a fit for you. It is often the way that our communities, including family and close friends, try to keep us in their circle, but it also leaves many of us trapped in a life that does not benefit us, or allow us to fulfill our potential.

I am here to tell you that it is possible to create a life that you are excited about, one where you can take risks that bring you greater rewards. My life is altered, and I am excited about the future because I opened my mind to the possibilities beyond operating heavy machinery. Now, I am an example to my daughter about pursuing her dreams, regardless of where they take her.

As you shift your mindset, choosing to buck the beliefs of others, you are going to find that you repel those that continue to have a negative frame of mind and start to attract those with a positive and open mindset.

Throughout my journey, I have made decisions based on what inspires and motivates me, not on a fear that I need to get back to work. I am not counting the days until I need to report back to work or let them know that I am not coming back. Instead, I am enjoying this adventure. I am excited to see where it leads me because I know, even though I am not there yet, I am closer than when I first started.

You cannot let fears, especially those of a financial kind, keep you from taking leaps. So many of the inspirational individuals in our world took leaps without a financial safety net. They didn't have an emergency fund or a set date when they would no longer pursue a goal if they weren't successful. They believed in acting to achieve their goals, no matter what financial challenges came their way. An unshakable desire to success. They adapted WIT in their lives, which stands for "WHATEVER IT TAKES."

I want you to take on a mentality that allows you to focus on achieving your goals and overcoming the challenges involved. When you give everything to your efforts, you will see them come to fruition. It starts with recognizing that the people you surround yourself with are going to push you to try harder and go further, or they will focus on trying to pull you down and break your spirit.

CREATE THE CIRCLE THAT SUPPORTS AND INSPIRES

The reason that I want to talk with you about the people you spend time with is that they are going to be part of those forces that influence you for good or bad. If you have specific goals that you want to achieve in life, then you need to surround yourself with those that will support you working to achieve those goals, while at the same time holding you accountable when you are working contrary to what you want to accomplish.

In the years since I moved to the mainland, I met someone who proved to be my biggest supporter and best friend, my dear love Amanda. As my significant other, she has the most influence in my world. If she had tried to stop me from pursuing my dreams, it might have meant the end of my journey. Instead, Amanda chose to step out in faith with me.

Without her, I do not believe I could have accomplished so much, so quickly. She stood by my side, took the leap with me, and our lives continue to blossom. She inspires me to never give up. I have found that surrounding myself with people who push me to be better and take chances are going to give me the fuel necessary to keep going, despite the challenges.

If you spend time with individuals that are not supportive, eventually you will give up. Your goals and dreams will remain unfulfilled and, years later, you will find yourself with regrets over what you should have done, instead of a sense of joy and accomplishment for what you have done. Remember, it is all about the influences that you allow in your life. Studies have shown that we become like the people that we spend the most time with. Who do you spend time with, and whose thoughts and ideas are you being exposed to on a regular basis? Do you have someone that you just know is in your corner that you are confident is adding value to your life?

It is easy to quit when you feel like you have no one in your corner. Amanda and I have been through many tough times, but the point is that we continue to stand together. You need to build that same type of support system, but also be willing to be that support system for others.

I want you to start focusing on how the people around you talk and act. Are they taking risks and inspiring others to follow their dreams? If not, you could be surrounding yourself with naysayers, those who are more likely to try to tear you down than build you up. If you want to make a change in your life, you need to first change your mindset, and then change who you spend your time with. After all, if you are changing your mindset, you need to spend time with individuals who will help you to reinforce that change.

Part of the way that I help myself to stay focused on a new open mindset is by choosing mentors that inspire me and give me critical food for thought. They help me to set my mind up for success. It is not about abandoning who I am, but recognizing that there is more to learn, to do, and more ways to grow as an individual who contributes to my culture and traditions. I also realized that they helped to set up my mindset to take even greater leaps and enjoy the opportunities that are available. It is not about the money, but about the fulfillment that comes from inspiring and being a role model for others from my community.

I choose to surround myself with mentors and associates that respect where I have come from, but who also challenge me to go further and to explore what the world has to offer. I want to leave a legacy for my family, but also to my people. I want them to recognize what is possible for ourselves and our nations. If you believe in yourself, you can achieve a lot in a short period of time, with or without a college education.

If you feel as if the darkness of life is overtaking you, I want you to stop and take an inventory of who you are surrounded by, and what type of encouragement they provide. You might find that they are taking light away and making the darkness appear that much worse.

The world is growing and changing constantly. We all have the wisdom born from our experiences, knowledge, and skills. Part of what makes us rich as human beings is the passing of that wisdom to others. When you find a mentor, you are finding a source of wisdom that you can tap into for your own benefit, and the benefit of those around you.

Start by looking for those that inspire you and then finding ways to interact with them. It could be through their writings or even their speeches. Use that inspiration to help motivate you to act. When you work with a mentor, you will find that you are pulled into their circle, and that will allow you to grow your circle with like-minded individuals who will help you to make the necessary changes to achieve your dreams.

I made some dramatic changes this past year, but much of that work started earlier. When I opened my mind to alternatives beyond the world I was living in, I started to believe I could act and create real change in my life. I saw the possibilities, and it was an exciting time. Still, I admit to having some fear and trepidation about whether I should actually move forward and take this leap into the unknown.

This is where your circle is so important. They will provide encouragement during those times of doubt, and when you wonder if you are truly capable of doing everything that you have ever imagined. Amanda provides that encouragement for me, and I like to think that I am just as supportive of her dreams. It is not a one-way street, but one built on mutual support.

Doubt is the enemy of those who want to build a different life, who see their purpose on a path that is not traditionally followed by those around them. You have the capacity to fight against that doubt by fueling yourself with positive thinking and gathering the tools you need to act.

What are some of those tools?

THE TOOLS THAT CAN INSPIRE YOU TO CREATE

I have already spoken about how important it is to create a circle that supports, encourages, and holds you accountable to create real change. This includes finding mentors and inspiring figures. You do not have to feel limited to just one mentor at a time. Mentors can be part of all aspects of your life, both personal and professional.

Depending on what you want to achieve, you may look for a specific type of mentor who has already walked that path. Over time, you may find yourself choosing another mentor because you have achieved your first goal and are now focused on another aspect of what you want to achieve, which requires help from another individual with experience and skills in that area.

My mentors were chosen because what they said inspired me, motivated me, and gave me food for thought. Remember, my world experience was fairly limited before I started down this path of life. Yet, once I got started, it helped me to reassess my life and understand that nothing was truly out of reach. I just had to act.

Another important tool is to find a means to keep yourself centered on your goals and objectives. The world has a way of naturally distracting us from our goals and objectives, simply because we are presented with challenging circumstances that can appear out of our control. Therefore, it is important to find ways to allow your mind to quiet, thus giving you the opportunity to refocus.

There are a variety of ways to do this. I know some individuals find that peace and clarity when they take the time to exercise daily. Others prefer meditation, taking the time out of the morning and evening to clear their minds through breathing exercises or other forms of meditation. Still others prefer time in nature, where they can reconnect with the air, soil, and animals that are part of our home.

Whatever your preferred method, I want you to make it a regular part of your routine. You can focus on the vision of your achievements, giving them life and very clear details. The point is to make them as rich as possible to make them as real as possible. When you focus on visualizing yourself successful in achieving your goals and endeavors, you will empower yourself to create. You can see yourself acting in a way to reach those goals, which serves as the inspiration to keep you moving forward.

Athletes use visualization techniques all the time to achieve their goals. Doing so, those athletes are inspired to keep up the thoughts and actions that will allow them to do what they want and achieve their goals. They have created a mindset that gives them the ability to be successful, no matter what challenges might come their way.

I find that visualization helps me to manifest my dreams and goals into my reality. The richer the detail, the sharper the image, the faster I can make it happen. Discussing these ideas and dreams with my partner also helps me to see it clearly in my mind. Ask yourself questions to help you flesh out all the details.

Our ancestors often gathered for ceremonies that allowed them to make decisions which guided their course. It was early visualization, and I want you to tap into that. No matter where we are from or how we were raised, we all have the power to create inside of us. Our connection with each other and the earth is what allows us to find success, regardless of the challenges that come our way.

We all have encountered mental quicksand in our lives. It comes in many forms, but we need to be vigilant in looking out for it and avoiding it wherever possible. If you find that you have fallen into a quicksand trap, then you need to stop for a moment, allowing yourself time to reset your mindset back on the path you want to take.

Those resets are not easy, but they can be done with mindful and conscious effort. Do not be quick to assume that just because you were distracted or pulled into that mental quicksand that you cannot pull yourself up and move forward. The fact of the matter is that you will have moments where you fall, where you feel doubt, and where you wonder if you really can be successful. I want you to recognize that when those moments come, you need to walk through them.

It will not always be easy, but it is necessary that you make a conscious effort to do so. It will help you to grow stronger and also give you the endurance necessary to achieve anything you want in life.

When I took my leave of absence, I truly did not know what was going to happen next. However, I left myself open to whatever possibilities presented themselves. Essentially, you have to train yourself not to immediately say no, but be willing to say yes, no matter how crazy or ill-prepared you might feel for the situation. I had to open my mind to the possibilities and be open to exploring what the world had to offer, without fear.

I believe that what you want to achieve in life, you have the power to attract. The universe will give to you what you focus on. If you focus on the positive aspects of a situation and the possibilities available to you, you will draw more opportunities to yourself. A path you might never have embarked on will open up right in front of you. It is this power that you need to tap to create a real directional shift in where your life is headed.

One of the effects of creating change for yourself is that you end up being able to impact others. After all, you do not live in a vacuum. While others are influencing you, you are influencing others.

Think of how great speakers can get you to think differently, can inspire you to act differently, and can chart a different course for various institutions. I want you to recognize that you have the same power within you. We all do!

I want you to be inspired to see the valuable person that you are and use that vision to create and build a future that can be a guidepost to others. There are so many ways to impact others. Like a ripple in a pond, those efforts can spread farther than you ever imagined! Here are just a few of the ones that can give others a jolt of inspiration and leave you with joy and love in your heart.

Volunteer – Do you know how many organizations need volunteers to achieve their missions? You could work with young people, old people, people who have been dealt horrible circumstances, those struggling to overcome an addiction to drugs or alcohol, and so much more. You have the power to influence their lives for the better, just by your presence and a willingness to listen. Always remember that whatever inspires you, there is likely an organization trying to move that agenda forward. Take part and recognize the gift you give when you give of yourself!

Invest – I am not just talking about finding the right financial investments. I mean invest in people. Be kind, be willing to forgive, and be willing to lend a hand. When we invest in each other, then we can create large-scale change. Jesus Christ is credited with saying there is more happiness in giving than in receiving. Give to others and see how it benefits your mindset and inspires you to keep those investments going.

Mentor – I also want you to recognize that you can serve as a mentor to others. It is a gift that keeps on giving, one that can allow you to pass down your wisdom to others. Mentoring is not a top-down affair. Someone that you mentor can also inspire you as well. Be open to the possibilities and you can truly be a gift to another individual looking to create change in their life.

As you can see, my life is in motion right now. I am writing, investing, and creating the life that I want, one that will allow me to care for my family and pursue those items on my bucket list. I chose to move away from a dark path based on the past choices of myself and others to create one that is filled with light and laughter. You don't have to be chained down to a way of living that leaves with a lifetime of regrets. Instead, I want you to focus on what is possible and then make it a reality.

There is no vision that is too great or too small for you to achieve. The biggest obstacle that you will ever have in your life is the one that you create by means of your mindset. When you choose a positive mindset, you are blasting that obstacle out of the water. Do not see risk as something to avoid, but rather as a means to achieve even more in your life.

I want to inspire you and help you to move forward in creating dramatic change in your life. I am always available via social media, and for those who know me, feel free to see how we can work together, how I can serve as a mentor, or even just share with you what inspires me to get out of bed and keep my focus.

I hope that you recognize that the darkness in your life does not have to win. You can let in the light and achieve more than you might have dreamed was possible. For those that need a boost, see my story as one that you can create for yourself. Recognize that I am just getting started. Your willingness to pick up this book means that you are ready to take a leap, and are just looking for the motivation. I hope I have provided that! May the life you want be manifested in your reality, and may you tap into your creative abilities.

"Use Your Struggles Today As Motivation For Tomorrow"

— Kirk Jakesta

Please visit Kirk Jakesta's website for more information, www.StreamLineToSuccess.com

Step Into Greatness

LES BROWN

You have greatness within you. You can do more than you could ever imagine. The problem most people have is that they set a goal and then ask, "how can I do it? I don't have the necessary skills or education or experience."

I know what that's like. I wasted 14 years on asking myself how I could be a motivational speaker. My mind focused on the negative—on the things that were in my way, rather than on the things that were not.

It's not what you don't have but what you think you need that keeps you from getting what you want from life. But, when the dream is big enough, the obstacles don't matter. You'll get there if you stay the course. Nothing can stop you but death itself.

Think about that last statement for a minute. There's nothing on this earth that can stop you from achieving what it is that you want. So, get out of your way, and quit sabotaging your dreams. Do everything in your power to make them happen—because you cannot fail!

They say the best way to die is with your loved ones gathered around your bed. But what if you were dying and it was the ideas you never acted upon, the gifts you never used and the dreams you never pursued, that were circled around your bed? Answer that question right now. Write down your answers. If you die this very moment, what ideas, what gifts, what dreams will die with you?

Then say: I refuse to die an unlived life! You beat out 40 million sperm to get here, and you'll never have to face such odds again. Walk through the field of life and leave a trail behind.

One day, one of my rich friends brought my mother a new pair of shoes for me. Now, even though we weren't well off, I didn't want them; they were a size nine and I was a size nine and a half. My mother didn't listen and told my sister to go get some Vaseline, which she rubbed all over my feet. Then my mother had me put those shoes on, minding that I didn't scrunch down the heel. She had my sister run some water in the bathtub, and I was told to get in and walk around in the water. I said that my feet hurt. She just ignored me and asked about my day at school, how everything went and did I get into any fights? I knew what she was up to, that she was trying to distract me, so I said I had only gotten into three fights. After a while mother asked me if my feet still hurt. I admitted that the pain had indeed lessened. She kept me walking in that tub until I had a brand new pair of comfortable, size nine and a half shoes.

You see, once the leather in the shoes got wet, they stretched! And what you need to do is stretch a little. I believe that most people don't set high goals and miss them, but rather, they set lower goals and hit them and then they stay there, stuck on the side of the highway of life. When you're pursuing your greatness, you don't know what your limitations are, and you need to act like you don't have any. If you shoot for the moon and miss, you'll still be in the stars.

You also need coaching (a mentor). Why? There are times you, too, will find yourself parked on the side of the highway of life with no gas in the vehicle. What you need then is someone to stop and offer to pick up some gas down the road a ways and bring it back to you. That person is your coach. Yes, they are there for advice, but their main job is to help you through the difficulties that life throws at all of us.

Another reason for having a coach is that you can't see the picture when you're in the frame. In other words, he or she can often see where you are with a clarity and focus that's unavailable to you. They're not going to leave you parked along the road of life, nor are they going to allow you to be stuck in the moment like a photo in a frame.

And let's say you just can't see your way forward. You don't believe it's possible. Sometimes you just have to believe in someone's belief in you. This could be your coach, a loved one, or even a staunch friend. You need to hear them say you can do it, time and again. Because, after all, faith comes from hearing and hearing and hearing.

Look at it this way. Most people fail because of possibility blindness. They can't see what lies before them. There are always possibilities. Because of this, your dream is possible. You may fail often. In fact, I want you to say this: I will fail my way to success. Here is why.

I had a TV show that failed. I felt I had to go back to public speaking. I had failed, so I parked my car for 10 years. Then I saw Dr. Wayne Dyer was still on PBS and I decided to call them. They said they would love to work with me and asked where I had been. I wasn't as good as I had been 10 years before, as I was out of practice, but I still had to get back in the game. I was determined to drive on empty.

Listen to recordings, go to seminars, challenge yourself, and you'll begin to step into your greatness; you'll begin to fill yourself with the energy you need to climb to greater heights. Most people never attend a seminar. They won't invest money in books or audio programs. You put yourself in the top five percent just by making a different choice than the average person. This is called contrary thinking. It's a concept taken from the financial industry. One considers choosing the exact opposite behaviour of the average person as a way to get better than average results. You don't have to make the contrarian choice, but if you don't have anything to lose by going that road, why not consider the option?

Make your move before you're ready. Walk by faith, not by sight, and make sure you're happy doing it. If you can't be happy, what else is there? Helen Keller said, "Life is short, eat the dessert first."

What is faith? Many of us think of God when we think of faith. A different viewpoint claims that faith is a firm belief in something for which there is no proof. I would rather think of faith as something that is believed especially with strong conviction. It is this last definition I am referring to when I say walk by faith, not by sight. Be happy and go forth with strong conviction that you are destined for greatness.

An important step on your way to greatness is to take the time to detoxify. You've got to look at the people in your life. What are they doing for you? Are they setting a pace that you can follow? If not, whose pace have you adjusted to? If you're the smartest in your group, find a new group.

Are the people in your life pulling you down or lifting you up? You know what to do, right? Banish the negative and stay with the positive; it's that simple. Dr. Norman Vincent Peale once said (when I was in the audience), "You are special. You have greatness within you, and you can do more than you could ever possibly imagine."

He overrode the inner conversations in my mind and reached the heart of me. He set me on fire. This is yet another reason for seeking out the help of a coach or mentor, or other new people in your life. They can do what Dr. Peale did for me. They can set your passion free.

How important is it to have the right kind of person/people on your side? There was a study done that determined it takes 16 people saying you can do something to overcome one person who says you can't do something. That's right, one negative, unsupportive person can wipe out the work of 16 other supportive people. The message can't be any clearer than that.

Let's face the cold, hard truth: most people stay in park along the highway of life. They never feel the passion, the love for their fellow man, or for the work they do. They are stuck in the proverbial rut. What's the reason? There are many reasons, but only one common factor: fear—fear of change, fear of failure, fear of success, fear they may not be good enough, fear of competition, even fear of rejection.

"Rejection is a myth," says Jack Canfield, co-author of The Chicken Soup for the Soul series. "It's not like you get a slap in the face each time you are rejected." Why not take every "no" you receive as a vitamin, and every time you take one, know you are another step closer to success.

You will win if you don't quit. Even a broken clock is right twice a day.

Professional baseball players, on average, get on base just three times out of every 10 times they face the opposing pitcher. Even superstars fail half of the time they appear at the plate.

Top commissioned salespeople face similar odds. They may make one sale from every three people they see, but it will have taken them between 75 and 100 telephone calls to make the 15 appointments they need to close their five sales for the week. And these are statistics for the elite. Most salespeople never reach these kinds of numbers.

People don't spend their lives working for just one company anymore. This means you must build up a set of skills and experiences that are portable. This can be done a number of ways, but my favorite approaches follow.

You must be willing to do the things others won't do, in order to have tomorrow the things that others don't have. Provide more service than you get paid for. Set some high standards for yourself.

Begin each day with your most difficult task. The rest of the day will seem more enjoyable and a whole lot easier.

Someone needs help with a problem? Be the solution to that problem.

Also, find those tasks that are being consistently ignored and do them. You'll be surprised by the results. An acquaintance of mine used this approach at a number of entry-level positions and each time he quickly ended up being offered a position in management.

You must increase your energy. Kick it up a notch. We are spirits having a physical existence; let your spirit shine. Quit frittering away your energy. Use it to move you closer to the achievement of your dreams. Refuse to spend it on non-productive activities.

What do people say about you when you leave a room? Are you willing to take responsibility—to walk your talk. There is a terrible epidemic sweeping our nation, and it is the refusal to take responsibility for one's actions. Consider that at some point in any situation there will have been a moment where you could have done something to change the outcome. To that end, you are responsible for what happened. It's a hard thing to accept, but it's true.

Life's hard. It was hard when I was told I had cancer. I had sunken into despair, and was hiding away in my study when my son came in. My son asked me if I was going to die. What could I do? I told him I was going to fight, even though I was scared. I also told him that I needed some help. Not because I was weak, but because I wanted to stay strong. Keep asking until you get help. Don't stop until you get it.

A setback is the setup for a comeback. A setback is simply a misstep on the long road of success. It means nothing in the larger scheme of things. And, surprisingly, it sets you up for your next win. It tends to focus you and your energy on your immediate goals, paving the way for your next sprint, for your comeback.

It's worth it. Your dreams are worth the sacrifices you'll have to make to achieve them. Find five reasons that will make your dreams worth it for you. Say to yourself, I refuse to live an unlived life.

If you are casual about your dreams, you'll end up a casualty. You must be passionate about your dreams, living and breathing them throughout your days. You've got to be hungry! People who are hungry refuse to take no for an answer. Make NO your vitamin. Be unstoppable. Be hungry. Let me give you an example of what I mean by hungry:

I decided I wanted to become a disc jockey, so I went down to the local radio station and asked the manager, Mr. Milton "Butterball" Smith, if he had a job available for a disc jockey. He said he did not. The next day I went back, and Mr. Smith asked, "Weren't you here yesterday?" I explained that I was just checking to see if anyone was sick or had died. He responded by telling me not to come back again. Day three, I went back again—with the same story. Mr. Smith told me to get out of there. I came back the fourth day and gave Mr. Smith my story one more time. He was so beside himself that he told me to get him a cup of coffee. I said, "Yes, sir!" That's how I became the errand boy.

While working as an errand boy at the station, I took every opportunity to hang out with the disc jockeys and to observe them working. After I had taught myself how to run the control room, it was just a matter of biding my time.

Then one day an opportunity presented itself. One of the disc jockeys by the name of Rockin' Roger was drinking heavily while he was on the air. It was a Saturday afternoon. And there I was, the only one there.

I watched him through the control-room window. I walked back and forth in front of that window like a cat watching a mouse, saying "Drink, Rock, Drink!" I was young. I was ready. And I was hungry.

Pretty soon, the phone rang. It was the station manager. He said, "Les, this is Mr. Klein."

I said, "Yes, I know."

He said, "Rock can't finish his program."

I said, "Yes sir, I know."

He said, "Would you call one of the other disc jockeys to fill in?"

I said, "Yes sir, I sure will, sir."

And when he hung up, I said, "Now he must think I'm crazy." I called up my mama and my girlfriend, Cassandra, and I told them, "Ya'll go out on the front porch and turn up the radio, I'M ABOUT TO COME ON THE AIR!"

I waited 15 or 20 minutes and called the station manager back. I said, "Mr. Klein, I can't find NOBODY!"

He said, "Young boy, do you know how to work the controls?"

I said, "Yes, sir."

He said, "Go in there, but don't say anything. Hear me?"

I said, "Yes, sir."

I couldn't wait to get old Rock out of the way. I went in there, took my seat behind that turntable, flipped on the microphone, and let 'er rip.

"Look out, this is me, LB., triple P. Les Brown your platter-playin' papa. There were none before me and there will be none after me, therefore that makes me the one and only. Young and single and love to mingle, certified, bona fide, and indubitably qualified to bring you satisfaction and a whole lot of action. Look out baby, I'm your LOVE man."

I WAS HUNGRY!

During my adult life, I've been a disc jockey, a radio station manager, a Democrat in the Ohio Legislature, a minister, a TV personality, an author, and a public speaker, but I've always looked after what I valued most—my mother. What I want for her is one of my dreams, one of my goals.

My life has been a true testament to the power of positive thinking and the infinite human potential. I was born in an abandoned building on a floor in Liberty City, a low-income section of Miami, Florida, and adopted at six weeks of age by Mrs. Mamie Brown, a 38-year-old single woman, cafeteria cook, and domestic worker. She had very little education or financial means, but a very big heart and the desire to care for myself and my twin brother. I call myself Mrs. Mamie Brown's Baby Boy and I say that all that I am and all that I ever hoped to be, I owe to my mother.

My determination and persistence in searching for ways to help my mother overcome poverty, and developing my philosophy to do whatever it takes to achieve success, led me to become a distinguished authority on harnessing human potential and success. That philosophy is best expressed by the following:

"If you want a thing bad enough to go out and fight for it,
to work day and night for it,
to give up your time, your peace, and your sleep for it...
if all that you dream and scheme is about it,
and life seems useless and worthless without it...
if you gladly sweat for it and fret for it and plan for it
and lose all your terror of the opposition for it...
if you simply go after that thing you want
with all of your capacity, strength, and sagacity,
faith, hope and confidence and stern pertinacity...
if neither cold, poverty, famine, nor gout,
sickness nor pain, of body, and brain,
can keep you away from the thing that you want...
if dogged and grim you beseech and beset it,
with the help of God, you will get it!"

The 3 Things You Need to Become a Real Estate Millionaire

The Right Way to Invest Successfully

RAYMOND AARON

It seems like everywhere you look, someone is claiming that they became a millionaire by investing in real estate, and encouraging you to do the same. There are lots of TV shows about flipping houses for a fast buck that make it appear as if it's easy to find the right property and just as easy to sell it in a matter of months for a good profit. Unfortunately, that's not really how it works.

Investing in real estate is a proven way to make money, a lot of it. You could end up with millions, but you could also make a lot of very costly mistakes along the way. There has been so much hype about how easy it is to become a real estate millionaire that many people jump into the market without knowing what they are doing, and that's a shame, especially because qualified help is available.

Anyone can invest successfully in real estate if they have three things: a great real estate mentor, a proven real estate system, and a way to correctly predict the future. In other words, you need someone smart and knowledgeable to guide you; an understanding of the financial and legal aspects of buying, holding, and selling real estate; and an ability to see societal trends and visualize how those trends will impact the real estate market.

A GREAT REAL ESTATE MENTOR

Investing on your own can be financially dangerous, especially for a first-timer. You're dealing with a lot of money, so any mistake can be a huge one. Buying at the wrong time in the cycle can kill your investments. And, regardless of the real estate strategy you employ, you're bound to hold onto properties for some period of time which means that severe negative cash flow and vacancies can ruin you. Plus, bad property management and a failure to know the most recent real estate and tax laws can get you sued.

An experienced mentor can help you choose the best real estate strategies for your situation, and the right properties in which to invest. They can also help you avoid the many possible pitfalls and make money while holding properties, and counsel you on when to sell for a great profit. Working with the right mentor can also keep real estate investing from becoming your full-time job.

Many people find that some part of the investment process is uncomfortable for them, whether it's initiating a conversation with a realtor, submitting an offer, or hiring a property manager. A mentor can be very helpful in such situations as well.

In sum, learning from and working with the right mentor can make you a highly profitable investor in a relatively short period of time. Look for someone with years of experience and a proven track record.

A PROVEN SYSTEM

There's much more to investing in real estate than "buy low, sell high." To be successful, you must have the correct facts and the correct monthly habits concerning your real estate. Overall, you need to know what to buy, when to buy it, whether there will be a positive cash flow while you're holding on to it, and when to sell. Plus, what is the right low? What is the right high? How much money do you have to put down and how much income must be generated while you're waiting to sell?

Determining if a property is a good buy takes a lot of research and analysis. You will need to look at comparable purchase prices in the area, as well as rental fees. You'll also need to consider the location, the age and condition of the building, tax rates, and about 30 other pieces of data. Evaluating the information for just one property could take you a day or more.

If you're serious about becoming a real estate investor, you are going to be considering quite a lot of properties on a regular basis. Even if you want to make investing your day job, you'll never have the time necessary to research fully and evaluate every property that comes to your attention. Hence, the first part of your system has to involve weeding out the lesser opportunities and focusing on the ones with potential.

The investors I mentor learn how to determine if a property is really a great deal in seconds. You only need two pieces of data: the purchase price and the current rent rate. Compare the two using a two-part formula. First, divide the asking price (outgoing funds) by 100. Then, given that current mortgage interest rates are below 8-10% divide the number you got by two. If the current monthly rent doesn't meet or better that second number, eliminate the property from consideration.

As an example, say the asking price is $1,000,000. If you divide it by 100, it comes out to $10,000. Divide again, by two, and you get $5,000. If the monthly rent isn't $5,000 or more, you should pass on the property. You may miss out on a few winners using this system but, if you eliminate more properties than you think you should, you'll be successful and safe. Remember that, if interest rates rise significantly, you will need to adjust the formula to compensate.

Once you've separated the chaff from the wheat, do your due diligence on the remaining properties. Work closely with your mentor during this part of the process and, again, when it comes to making deals, say no more than you say yes. Just don't get cold feet or shy away from a great deal.

In terms of timing, it all comes down to momentum. There is always an overall upward momentum. Real estate prices go up and down, on an upwards track. So, one good profit strategy is to buy low, watch values rise and sell during the next boom. More precisely, you want to buy just as prices rise off the bottom (so that they're already rising) and sell when prices hit double the bottom, which is typically the very minimum prices rise to at the peak of the ensuing boom.

Don't attempt to predict the extremes—you will make a significant amount of money more safely buying just after prices begin rising (not the lowest point) and selling towards the end of the up period—without the risk associated with waiting too long and missing the highest point.

You'll also need a system for monitoring your investments while holding on until it's time to sell. Having a strong property manager is essential. So is reviewing rents taken in versus uncollectibles, repairs, and other expenses to ensure that your cash flow remains positive.

PREDICTING THE FUTURE

Good real estate investors learn to identify marketplace trends and buyers' or renters' needs. Start by investigating and tracking growth trends by neighborhood: are prices rising, is an area getting ready for a renaissance, are there new job opportunities nearby, or is the area close to another neighborhood that's gotten too pricey?

Great real estate investors, however, go far beyond those basics. They look for large demographic or social elements that might provide the next big opportunity. The huge number of returning veterans after World War II led to a Baby Boom that provides the perfect example. Every stage of their lives brought an opportunity for marketers, real estate builders, and other manufacturers to fill unmet needs, be it starter homes for when they had children, tricycles for those children who were too young to ride a bike, or new sizes and types of cars. All of this was predictable, but no one noticed. Opportunities were capitalized upon as they arose, but imagine what financial success could have been attained if someone had predicted the Baby Boomers' needs in advance.

And, now, those Boomers are driving the growth of retirement communities and nursing homes. But, they are a more independent lot than their parents were, and have strived to remain young and healthy as long as possible. Quite a few of them can still live and thrive on their own, but many may need a little help at this point in their lives. They don't need or want an aide, nurse, or social worker on a full-time basis, and certainly aren't ready for a nursing home. That means there is a huge need for more up-to-date, internet-ready independent supportive living arrangements, of which there are too few. Investing in one now is bound to be a win.

Don't forget that those Baby Boomers had children of their own, and that created a mini baby boom. Think about the ways in which those children, now middle-aged adults, are different from their parents and what needs they might have, especially regarding real estate. You might also consider whether changes in the workforce, higher divorce rates, and the economics of leaving home after college have implications for the real estate market as well. Keep your eyes and minds open!

Happiness: How to Experience the "Real Deals"

MARCI SHIMOFF

I was 41 years old, stretched out on a lounge chair by my pool and reflecting on my life. I had achieved all that I thought I needed to be happy.

You see, when I was a child, I thought there would be five main things that would ensure that I'd be happy: a successful career helping people, a loving husband, a comfortable home, a great body, and a wonderful circle of friends. After years of study, hard work, and a few "lucky breaks," I finally had them all. (Okay, so my body didn't quite look like Halle Berry's—but four out of five isn't bad!) You think I'd have been on the top of the world.

But surprisingly I wasn't. I felt an emptiness inside that the outer successes of life couldn't fill. I was also afraid that if I lost any of those things, I might be miserable. Sadly, I knew I wasn't alone in feeling this way.

While happiness is the one thing we all truly want, so few people really experience the deep and lasting fulfillment that fills our soul. Why aren't we finding it?

Because, in the words of the old country western song, we're looking for happiness in "all the wrong places."

Looking around, I saw that the happiest people I knew weren't the most successful and famous. Some were married, some were single. Some had lots of money, and some didn't have a dime. Some of them even had health challenges. From where I stood, there seemed to be no rhyme or reason to what made people happy. The obvious question became: *Could a person actually be happy for no reason?*

I had to find out.

So I threw myself into the study of happiness. I interviewed scores of scientists, as well as 100 unconditionally happy people. (I call them the Happy 100.) I delved into the research from the burgeoning field of positive psychology, the study of the positive traits that enable people to enjoy meaningful, fulfilling, and happy lives.

What I found changed my life. To share this knowledge with others, I wrote a book called *Happy for No Reason: 7 Steps to Being Happy from the Inside Out.*

One day, as I sat down to compile my findings, all the pieces of the puzzle fell into place. I had a simple, but profound "a-ha"—there's a continuum of happiness.

Unhappy	Happy for Bad Reason	Happy for Good Reason	Happy for No Reason
↕	↕	↕	↕
Depressed	High from unhealthy addictions	Satisfaction from healthy experiences	Inner state of peace & well-being

EXTERNAL   INTERNAL

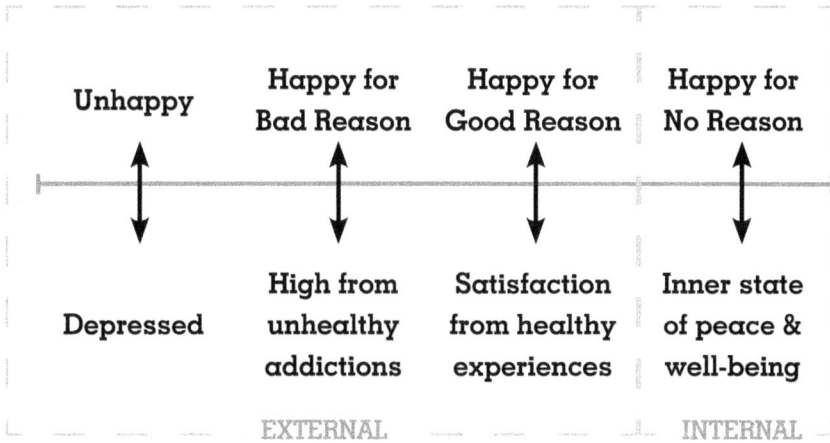

Unhappy: We all know what this means: life seems flat. Some of the signs are anxiety, fatigue, feeling blue or low—your "garden-variety" unhappiness. This isn't the same as clinical depression, which is characterized by deep despair and hopelessness that dramatically interferes with your ability to live a normal life, and for which professional help is absolutely necessary.

Happy for Bad Reason: When people are unhappy, they often try to make themselves feel better by indulging in addictions or behaviors that may feel good in the moment but are ultimately detrimental. They seek the highs that come from drugs, alcohol, excessive sex, "retail therapy," compulsive gambling, over-eating, and too much television-watching, to name a few. This kind of "happiness" is hardly happiness at all. It is only a temporary way to numb or escape our unhappiness through fleeting experiences of pleasure.

Happy for Good Reason: This is what people usually mean by happiness: having good relationships with our family and friends, success in our careers, financial security, a nice house or car, or using our talents and strengths well. It's the pleasure we derive from having the healthy things in our lives that we want.

Don't get me wrong. I'm all for this kind of happiness! It's just that it's only half the story. Being Happy for Good Reason depends on the external conditions of our lives—if these conditions change or are lost, our happiness usually goes too. Relying solely on this type of happiness is where a lot of our fear is stemming from these days. We're afraid the things we think we need to be happy may be slipping from our grasp.

Deep inside, I think we all know that life isn't meant to be about getting by, numbing our pain, or having everything "under control." True happiness doesn't come from merely collecting an assortment of happy experiences. At our core, we know there's something more than this.

There is. It's the next level on the happiness continuum—Happy for No Reason.

Happy for No Reason: This is true happiness—a state of peace and well-being that isn't dependent on external circumstances.

Happy for No Reason isn't elation, euphoria, mood spikes, or peak experiences that don't last. It doesn't mean grinning like a fool 24/7 or experiencing a superficial high. Happy for No Reason isn't an emotion. In fact, when you are Happy for No Reason, you can have *any* emotion—including sadness, fear, anger, or hurt—but you still experience that underlying state of peace and well-being.

When you're Happy for No Reason, you *bring* happiness to your outer experiences rather than trying to *extract* happiness from them. You don't need to manipulate the world around you to try to make yourself happy. You live *from* happiness, rather than *for* happiness.

This is a revolutionary concept. Most of us focus on being Happy for Good Reason, stringing together as many happy experiences as we can, like beads in a necklace, to create a happy life. We have to spend a lot of time and energy trying to find just the right beads so we can have a "happy necklace."

Being Happy for No Reason, in our necklace analogy, is like having a happy string. No matter what beads we put on our necklace—good, bad, or indifferent—our inner experience, which is the string that runs through them all, is happy, and creates a happy life.

Happy for No Reason is a state that's been spoken of in virtually all spiritual and religious traditions throughout history. The concept is universal. In Buddhism, it is called causeless joy; in Christianity, the kingdom of Heaven within; and in Judaism it is called *ashrei*, an inner sense of holiness and health. In Islam it is called *falah*, happiness and well-being; and in Hinduism it is called *ananda*, or pure bliss. Some traditions refer to it as an enlightened or awakened state.

So how can you be Happy for No Reason?

Science is verifying the way. Researchers in the field of positive psychology have found that we each have a "happiness set-point," that determines our level of happiness. No matter what happens, whether it's something as exhilarating as winning the lottery or as challenging as a horrible accident, most people eventually return to their original happiness level. Like your weight set-point, which keeps the scale hovering around the same number, your happiness set-point will remain the same **unless you make a concerted effort to change it.** In the same way you'd crank up the thermostat to get comfortable on a chilly day, you actually have the power to reprogram your happiness set-point to a higher level of peace and well-being. The secret lies in practicing the habits of happiness.

Some books and programs will tell you that you can simply decide to be happy. They say just make up your mind to be happy—and you will be.

I don't agree.

You can't just decide to be happy, any more than you can decide to be fit or to be a great piano virtuoso and expect instant mastery. You can, however, decide to take the necessary steps, like exercising or taking piano lessons—and by practicing those skills, you can get in shape or give recitals. In the same way, you can become Happy for No Reason through practicing the habits of happy people.

All of your habitual thoughts and behaviors in the past have created specific neural pathways in the wiring in your brain, like grooves in a record. When we think or behave a certain way over and over, the neural pathway is strengthened and the groove becomes deeper—the way a well-traveled route through a field eventually becomes a clear-cut path. Unhappy people tend to have more negative neural pathways. This is why you can't just ignore the realities of your brain's wiring and *decide* to be happy! To raise your level of happiness, you have to create new grooves.

Scientists used to think that once a person reached adulthood, the brain was fairly well "set in stone" and there wasn't much you could do to change it. But new research is revealing exciting information about the brain's neuroplasticity: when you think, feel, and act in different ways, the brain changes and actually rewires itself. You aren't doomed to the same negative neural pathways for your whole life. Leading brain researcher Dr. Richard Davidson, of the University of Wisconsin says, "Based on what we know of the plasticity of the brain, we can think of things like happiness and compassion as skills that are no different from learning to play a musical instrument or tennis ... it is possible to train our brains to be happy."

While a few of the Happy 100 I interviewed were born happy, most of them learned to be happy by practicing habits that supported their happiness. That means wherever you are on the happiness continuum, it's entirely in your power to raise your happiness level.

In the course of my research, I uncovered 21 core happiness habits that anyone can use to become happier and stay that way. You can find all 21 happiness habits at www.HappyForNoReason.com.

Here are a few tips to get you started:

1. **Incline your mind toward joy.** Have you noticed that your mind tends to register the negative events in your life more than the positive? If you get 10 compliments in a day and one criticism, what do you remember? For most people, it's the criticism. Scientists call this our "negativity bias"—our primitive survival wiring that causes us to pay more attention to the negative than the positive. To reverse this bias, get into the daily habit of consciously registering the positive around you: the sun on your skin, the taste of a favorite food, a smile or kind word from a co-worker or friend. Once you notice something positive, take a moment to savor it deeply and feel it; make it more than just a mental observation. Spend 20 seconds soaking up the happiness you feel.

2. **Let love lead.** One way to power up your heart's flow is by sending loving kindness to your friends and family, as well as strangers you pass on the street. Next time you're waiting for the elevator at work, stuck in a line at the store or caught up in traffic, send a silent wish to the people you see for their happiness, well-being, and health. Simply wishing others well switches on the "pump" in your own heart that generates love and creates a strong current of happiness.

3. **Lighten your load.** To make a habit of letting go of worries and negative thoughts, start by letting go on the physical level. Cultural anthropologist Angeles Arrien recommends giving or throwing away 27 items a day for nine days. This deceptively simple practice will help you break attachments that no longer serve you.

4. **Make your cells happy.** Your brain contains a veritable pharmacopeia of natural happiness-enhancing neurochemicals—endorphins, serotonin, oxytocin, and dopamine—just waiting to be released to every organ and cell in your body. The way that you eat, move, rest, and even your facial expression can shift the balance of your body's feel-good-chemicals, or "Joy Juice," in your favor. To dispense some extra Joy Juice—smile. Scientists have discovered that smiling decreases stress hormones and boosts happiness chemicals, which increase the body's T-cells, reduce pain, and enhance relaxation. You may not feel like it, but smiling—even artificially to begin with—starts the ball rolling and will turn into a real smile in short order.

5. **Hang with the happy.** We catch the emotions of those around us just like we catch their colds—it's called emotional contagion. So it's important to make wise choices about the company you keep. Create appropriate boundaries with emotional bullies and "happiness vampires" who suck the life out of you. Develop your happiness "dream team"—a mastermind or support group you meet with regularly to keep you steady on the path of raising your happiness.

"Happily ever after" isn't just for fairytales or for only the lucky few. Imagine experiencing inner peace and well-being as the backdrop for everything else in your life. When you're Happy for No Reason, it's not that your life always looks perfect—it's that, however it looks, you'll still be happy!

By Marci Shimoff. Based on the New York Times bestseller *Happy for No Reason: 7 Steps to Being Happy from the Inside Out*, which offers a revolutionary approach to experiencing deep and lasting happiness. The woman's face of the *Chicken Soup for the Soul* series and a featured teacher in *The Secret*, Marci is an authority on success, happiness, and the law of attraction. To order *Happy for No Reason* and receive free bonus gifts, go to www.happyfornoreason.com/mybook.

Unlocking the Secret to Success

Discovering the Power of Emotional Intelligence

RAV BAINS

WHAT IS EMOTIONAL INTELLIGENCE?

What is an emotion?

An emotion is a feeling we get as a result of something that has triggered us. This trigger can be internal or external; in other words, something that we think, see, hear, speak or do. For example, you might see two people arguing, and that could arouse some emotion in you. An example of an internal trigger could be that you think of something in the past that was negative, and this has brought up an emotion in you. The other important factor to remember is that an emotion can be strong or weak. The strength of the emotion will depend on your interpretation of what you've thought, seen, heard, spoke or done. Since we all have different values and belief systems, the event, whether internal or external, is "neutral." Why is this important to understand? Because you have a choice as to how to react to the thing that has happened! Now you might ask how this is possible. If I see a car accident how can that be neutral? Isn't it bound to evoke an emotion? Well, what is the likelihood that ten people who witnessed the accident will have the same reaction? They won't. Their reactions could range from very strong to slight, to no reaction at all. So, it's not the event, but rather your interpretation of that event that will determine the emotion. One of the reasons you blame the event for your emotional reaction is that it all happens in a fraction of a second! As a result, you confuse the trigger (the event) with your emotional reaction, which is actually determined by you. This topic always becomes an interesting conversational point in my seminars, which is great because it allows for rich understanding of emotions and triggers. The important thing to remember is that life has no meaning until we give it meaning.

What triggers an emotion?

Now that we have touched on emotions and triggers, the next critical question for you to ask is what triggers your emotions. Understanding this question is fundamental to understanding your personal and professional success or failure. You see, people never stop to think why they have an emotional reaction to something. In fact, did you know that 90% of the population don't think? (Earl Nightingale) Just because they have thoughts (which are often haphazard), they believe they are thinking. Thinking is the deliberate, conscious awareness of the thoughts you are having, and deciding what thoughts you actually want to have. The other fundamental mistake people make is that they think they are their thoughts. We aren't our thoughts. We are aware of our thoughts, so we can't be the thoughts. Now at this point you might feel a little confused.

That's ok, it will become clearer as you read on. It's critical that you get to know what triggers you. It could be what people say or do, or certain circumstances, situations or events. It's also important to be aware of the type of emotion or feeling you're getting in those situations and circumstances. These emotions will determine how you act and react. Are they positive or negative? Are they pleasurable or painful? These questions will help to determine whether you're making good judgments or not. They will also determine whether you're responding or reacting to the person, situation or circumstances. One of the other fundamental factors to remember is that human beings can trigger an emotional reaction simply by thinking bad thoughts—without anyone else interfering. So, you can get into a bad mood all by yourself!

Emotions drive behavior

Many people seem to think that their circumstances cause them to react to things, and

that's why they have an emotional reaction. As a result, they constantly blame what's happening around them, which is external to them. In my coaching sessions I've heard so many individuals complain about their partner, the kids, the boss or their team at work. It's as if they think that changing what's around them will allow them to be happy or in a better mood. This means no more emotional reaction. Well, if you've been following the earlier reading, then you'll have remembered that all events are neutral, and only you are in control of your feelings and emotions. Therefore, the mood you're in or the emotional reaction you're having to a situation or event will determine how you behave! For example, if you're in a bad mood, what's the likelihood you're going to be at your best at home or in the workplace? We can safely assume you're not going to be! What many people fail to realize is that emotions, not circumstances, drive behavior. So, how you're feeling or what kind of emotional state you're in will determine your performance and your leadership. This means that if you want to change your own or someone else's behavior you must get to the root cause of the emotion that's driving them or you, otherwise you'll be focusing your energies on the symptoms instead of causes and, as a result, be less effective in your efforts. This is one of the key elements to understand as part of EI.

Definition of EI

Now that we've established what emotions are, what triggers emotions and that emotions drive behavior, we can conclude that *EI is one's ability to understand one's emotions—what triggers them, what circumstances cause the trigger and how to regulate the emotions.* By doing this there is a good chance that you'll make better, more thoughtful decisions and have a positive impact on those around you. This means better performance by you, and the role modeling of good personal leadership.

WHAT IS WISDOM?

Wisdom is having the knowledge of what is right or true, coupled with just judgment regarding an action to be taken. The most famous example of this is the story of two women who came to King Solomon, each claiming to be the mother of a certain infant. Knowing that only one could be the true mother,

King Solomon decreed that the baby be cut in half and one part given to each woman. The true mother, unwilling to have her baby hurt in any way, revoked her claim. Solomon knew this would happen and, thus, awarded the child to that woman.

Intelligence versus Wisdom

King Solomon had to understand intelligence in order to make the decision he did … He had to be prepared to go through with his decree. And he also had to know how the true mother would react. So, on the surface, it would seem that both intelligence and emotional intelligence are necessary for wisdom. However, if we accept that the two women were intelligent in their own way, it quickly becomes apparent that intelligence is not necessary for wisdom.

Why is this important?

Thinking is the deliberate, conscious awareness of the thoughts you're having and then deciding what thoughts you want to have. This is the exact opposite of what most people do. Most people base their actions on how they feel in the moment. They don't take time to rationalize the situation and choose an appropriate thought.

WHY DO ORGANIZATIONS NEED EMOTIONAL INTELLIGENCE?

Because there are:

- **Challenges in individual behavior** … Once Emotional Intelligence is understood by individuals in organizations, their behavior changes dramatically. They stop reacting and start to respond thoughtfully to situations.

- **Challenges in building relationships** ... If employees are unable to cooperate with each other, this will affect organizational performance. Once people start to grasp the concept and competences of self-awareness, cooperation and harmony, it will lead to better results.

- **Challenges in teamwork** ... Teamwork is critical for success; however, too often individuals in teams fall into the "right wrong trap!" and individuals quickly start to take positions. Once people understand that it's all emotional, they start to focus on outcomes and results.

- **Challenges in managing change** ... Organizations struggle in implementing change, and employees often resist. Fear is a big factor in change management, as people focus on what they will lose as opposed to what they will gain. People start to 'awfulize,' but once they understand that it's the relationship between the emotional mind and the thinking mind that is driving the fear, resistance disappears.

- **Challenges in achieving organizational goals** ... Employees often struggle with their values versus the organization's values. They often forget what their Personal Leadership Responsibility is in the organization. Understanding the philosophy of Emotional Intelligence and personal accountability puts them back on the right track.

- **Challenges in understanding 'soft skills!'** ... Organizations spend millions of dollars on driving hard for goals and results, but remain weak on developing the soft skills required by individuals and teams. They fail to realize that it's the 'soft stuff' that makes the 'hard stuff' easier! Once individuals and teams grasp this concept, they excel in all areas of their lives and get engaged actively in achieving organizational results.

The main thing to remember about Emotional Intelligence is that it can be taught, improved and used within your company to create a healthy workplace, motivate employees and achieve your goals. It's definitely a strong tool that can put you out in front of your competition. So, get from being a good organization to a great organization!

UNDERSTANDING EMOTIONS AS VIBRATIONS

One of the failures of our learning is that no one has explained to us that emotions are actual vibrations in the body. When we are angry, we don't say "I have a negative vibration" we say "I am angry!" In other words, we have made the emotion part of who we are and, as a result, we do not pay attention to the vibration. We don't realize that it's a vibration, and that we aren't our vibrations. We are aware of our vibrations. I know this might be a little confusing, BUT this is one of the keys to really grasping what is happening to us emotionally. As a result, we'll have a chance to manage our emotions and hence our behavior.

It's critical to be in tune with what is happening in the body, and paying attention when there is a change in this vibration, because then you'll know you're having a reaction to something. I can't stress enough the importance of this fact. Start paying attention to the sensations/vibrations in your body. Stop living from the neck upwards, just in the mind!

I believe you aren't going to get this important piece of information from any other emotional intelligence book or trainer.

THINK ABOUT WHAT YOU'RE THINKING

We very rarely pay any attention to our thoughts. The average person doesn't understand the importance of thinking. People assume this is an activity that just happens and that they really don't have any control over it. Wrong! If you want to change your life, then start paying attention to what you're constantly thinking about. Are your thoughts negative or positive? Why is this important? Well, thoughts arouse emotions. Earl Nightingale, in 1960, said that "90% of people simply don't think!" You see, you need to understand that activity in the mind isn't thinking. We're constantly thinking about shopping lists, work, picking the kids up, cooking, and on and on we go! Not that this isn't important, but you need to understand that you're not your thoughts. You are, however, aware of your thoughts and therefore can choose what you think about. Negative thoughts will trigger negative emotions. Conversely, positive thoughts will trigger positive emotions, which in turn puts us in a better state of mind. We as humans have so habituated negative thinking that we have normalized it. So we pay no attention to what we're thinking and how it is affecting our behavior and performance. Understanding the importance of your thoughts, which give rise to emotions, is critical in changing your behavior. Managing your thinking and your emotions will lead to better management of your behavior. Remember, thoughts arouse emotions.

What is thinking?

Thinking is conscious and it's active. Think of it as internal speech (requires language). Sometimes that inner conversation appears to come unbidden or automatically; this would be subconscious thought. But it is during conscious and active thought that thinking takes on a whole new role. Here we can focus our thoughts to solve a problem. We can plan, design and, quite literally, create. This is where we can purposefully produce our thoughts and put some form to them. In simpler words, thinking is the action of using one's mind to produce thoughts.

90% of the people don't think

It's true; most people don't think. They go through their days on automatic, their thoughts being a reaction to what's happening around them and to them, rather than being a purposeful response. No wonder, though. The Socratic method is no longer taught in schools, and the young people of today don't seem to understand the importance of the "question." If you ask yourself (your mind) a question, the mind will always answer. Ask a great question, and you'll always get a great response. In fact, it's the act of questioning that creates our thoughts. So, think what will happen to a person who doesn't understand the importance of questions. Something happens, and random, or at least reactive, thoughts appear. Negative questions abound. *Why is this happening to me? What's going on? Who does he think he is? Where does this leave me?* Get the picture? What if this person had responded rather than reacted? The questions asked might appear like this: *This is interesting: how can what's happening serve me? Do I understand the situation properly, or will he clarify it for me? He certainly has some strong opinions: I wonder what his experience is in this area and if he would be interested in sharing his story and his reasoning? I think I'll ask him. Can't hurt, right?*

Why is this important?

The questions we ask will determine what we say and do. They are like the programs we feed our computer so that it can manipulate the raw data it receives in a way that is useful to us. You're the operator or programmer of your mind. You don't want to fall asleep on the job, do you? Then learn to ask yourself questions designed to get your mind used to generating specific words and actions so that they become a habit you can call on in many different situations. I call them rituals.

Thoughts arouse emotions

One of the most wonderful aspects of thought is that it can arouse emotions. You can discover which words or thoughts elicit emotions that can work for you in a difficult situation, then you can practice calling up those emotions. I'm talking about positive emotions like excitement, joy, happiness, and peace.

COMPETENCES OF EMOTIONAL INTELLIGENCE

There are many different views and opinions on the competences of Emotional Intelligence. I've found the following to be the best examples to describe the important competences.

Self-awareness is the foundation on which all other competences build on. Often, we don't take the time to disengage from day-to-day activity to review what has happened to us.

Example ... Before you go to bed at night, take the time to review your day. Ask questions like: *What were the positives? Which of my goals were achieved? What happened to make the day memorable?* Once you feel your review is complete, set your mind to work, planning tomorrow's day. You should write your goals down.

Example ... How can you really understand your stress levels if you don't spend some quiet time posing and answering questions designed to put your focus on the stress you feel in each large muscle mass? So, think back to a time when you felt totally relaxed and the stress literally bled from your body. What did that feel like? Compare that feeling to the one in the muscle mass we've been talking about. Clench those muscles for a count of ten and release. Does the feeling in the muscles match what you remembered? Not quite? Clench the muscles for another 10 seconds and release. Immediately notice how the muscles feel. Now do this with all the large muscles in your body, beginning with your head and working downward to your feet.

Make sure you're doing your best to match the feeling of relaxation you remembered. Breathe in when you clench, breathe out when you release. You can even pretend you're releasing the air through the muscle you just released. Do you feel yourself settling into your chair or your bed? Keep practicing and one day soon you'll find yourself completely relaxed.

Self-assessment is the ability to honestly assess one's strengths and weakness. This has to be done skillfully. It's an opportunity to review what you're naturally good at and what the opportunities are for self-improvement. Self-assessment does not mean beating yourself up! But, rather, it's thoughtful self-reflection that adds value in increasing your awareness about yourself and how you interact with your environment.

Again, use questions to elicit the thoughts you're after. *What did I do well today? What skills and talents did I use? What could I have done better? How?*

Managing Emotion

I've heard emotion referred to as a wild stallion that must be tamed. Thoughts generate emotions; emotions generate thoughts. Of the two possibilities, which seems more useful to you? Thoughts generating emotions, right? You have the reins: it's up to you to teach the stallion what that means, that you're in control.

It's much easier to choose useful thoughts that generate positive, supporting emotions than it is to control the thoughts evoked by powerful, negative emotions. Think about it ... you always have a choice. You can ask questions that create thoughts that will evoke useful emotions or you can be overrun by thoughts that boil up unbidden from out of control negative emotion. You can tame the wild stallion or it can cast you into the dirt.

How is this emotion working for me? What thoughts can I choose that will evoke a better emotional response? What's good about this situation, and how can it serve me? Such questions are designed to focus on positive thoughts, emotions and results rather than reacting blindly to whatever emotion is elicited by the situation at hand.

Emotional Intelligence can be taught, improved and used within your company to achieve your goals. It is definitely a strong tool that can put you out in front of your competition. For more information or to book a seminar for your company, contact me at **ravsbains1@gmail.com**.

FINAL NOTE

The most important thing you can take away from this chapter is: **Life has no meaning other than what we give it**. A woman at a party stumbles and falls. One person is concerned that the woman might have been hurt by the fall. A second person starts laughing (because he noticed that the contents of the woman's drink flew into the face of someone he doesn't like very much).

In this situation, a woman fell. This has no meaning without context, hence the reactions of the two witnesses. They both put the fall into a specific context and then assigned meaning. The first witness saw the fall in the context of the woman becoming injured. This triggered the emotion of concern. The second witness saw the fall in the context of someone he disliked getting a drink in the face. This triggered the emotion of delight.

The trick, the wisdom we must develop, is understanding that we have FREE WILL to choose whatever it is we want to think, feel, say or do. It doesn't matter what has happened, because it means nothing until, and if, we make it so.

Remember ... "People will often forget what you said, but they will never forget how you made them feel." - Maya Angelou

To book a seminar for your organization, contact
Rav Bains at **ravsbains1@gmail.com**

Never Give Up!

My Journey to Purpose

VIVIAN STARK

NEVER GIVE UP: GROWTH AND SUCCESS COME IN INCREMENTS, NOT LEAPS

My desire is to encourage you with my life story. I have spent my life learning and improving myself, and I am thrilled to share what I have learned with you. Today I am living my definition of success. I have said NO TO THE PITY PARTY! Personal growth and development are a daily diet staple, and have fueled me in my business and entrepreneurial successes.

I wake up every day, knowing I am living my life with purpose, knowing I am the kind of person I always wanted to be. I have faced many challenges; my story has failures as well as successes. But I have learned that setbacks are only a part of the story; they are not the whole story. The story keeps going as long as you keep trying. You can choose to quit and make the story end in failure or dissatisfaction, or you can choose to keep trying and make your story what you want it to be.

Never give up. Success and growth do not come in leaps, they come in increments. The challenges will keep coming at you and sometimes it feels like two steps forward, one step back. But remember you did have those steps forward and you will again – if you never give up. You can choose to be overcome by dreck that life throws at you, or you can open your eyes to the love and opportunity that are always there too. You can have the life you want if you never, never, never give up on what is important – You.

IT IS YOUR LIFE - LIVE IT YOUR WAY

My life is my own for the making, but I did not always know this. I lived a very sheltered life as a child, fiercely protected by my overbearing Greek parents. I was not allowed to do the 'normal' girl things, like have sleepovers or join the Girl Guides to be a Brownie. When I was older I was not allowed to date for fear of gossip within my community. My parents lived in fear of the unknown. I lived in fear of being reprimanded if I disobeyed.

Despite my fear, insecurity, and extremely introverted personality, I pushed myself to exert my independence and fulfill certain goals that I set out for myself. From a very young age, I felt that I always needed to prove myself. To prove that I was pretty enough, smart enough, or even good enough. I worked tirelessly to achieve my dreams, never sharing them with anyone for fear of being ridiculed.

I began pursuing my goals as a young teen who wanted to fit in. I lived in an affluent area of Vancouver and always felt out of place. I did not have all the cool clothes that everyone else had, so I worked with my brother as a gardener cutting grass for one of my dad's clients. I saved my money and bought the clothes I wanted so that I would 'fit in' with the crowd. Despite this, I never felt that I fit in with other kids.

I was a rather "ugly duckling" as a younger girl, with a massive overbite and awkward shyness about me. After having braces, I felt my "ugly" stage was behind me and I decided to take a modeling class over several weeks one summer when I was in high school. My parents did not support me in this decision, so I chose to pay for it myself. The modeling class cost $800. I worked at Zellers for $3.00/hour. I persevered and saved enough money to pay for the class.

It turns out that the modeling class was just what I needed. I learned how to carry myself and exude confidence. After finishing the class, I took several modeling jobs and had many successes in my short modeling career. I made the cover of the then prestigious Back to School catalog for Eaton's Department Store, along with several other fun and exciting modeling adventures.

My modeling highlight and a fond memory was when I was hired for a ski catalog. (They wanted a curvy model. Who knew that sometimes it pays to not be super skinny!) We were taken up to the top of Blackcomb Mountain by helicopter before the official ski season opening. I remember having to jump out of the helicopter into three feet of snow because the helipad was snow-covered, and the helicopter could not land. I was paid $850 per day for three days. It was a dream come true. I felt validated.

When I was nineteen I began dating a handsome Greek guy I met at a wedding. Before I knew it, his parents and my parents got together and began planning our wedding. I literally cannot remember him actually asking me to marry him. How sad is that? Some time before our wedding I found out that he was into drugs and was still seeing his ex-girlfriend. I broke up with him and cancelled the wedding.

To escape well-meaning friends and relatives, I took an extended holiday to Greece where I could recover from the breakup. Armed with my modeling composite cards and my lovely, fashionable clothes, I hoped to land some modeling jobs while I was there. Instead, I met another handsome Greek guy who was smooth and charming. He swept me off my feet.

In classic old-school Greek fashion, my mom flew to Greece to check him out and determine whether he was a suitable partner for me. Like I said, I lived a sheltered life. She approved and, after a civil wedding in Canada, I moved to Greece to start my life with my new husband.

The first thing he did when we settled in to our home was give away all my beloved clothes. He proceeded to tell me what I could and could not do, where I could and could not go, and how I had to act. He, like my parents, was consumed with what other people thought of him and now me. I was terrified. What had I done?

I realized very quickly I had made a huge mistake and wanted to leave him and go back to Canada. To my surprise, I was already pregnant. Too embarrassed to tell anyone my sad state of affairs, I stayed in Greece. I had made an agreement with my husband that our children would be born in Canada. I did not want to risk my children having to go to the army if they were boys. After my first son was born, I returned to Greece.

When I became pregnant with my second son, I decided to leave Greece, not to return. I told my husband I was going back to Canada and he could come with me or not. He chose to move to Canada with me, but we broke up after a few years. Our marriage was just not meant to be, but I was blessed with two healthy, adorable and rambunctious boys that I loved so much.

Once divorced, my husband went back to Greece to avoid paying child support and to be near his momma, so she could pamper and take care of him. (It's a Greek thing. He was a huge momma's boy. Never again.) I was determined that my two boys would never be momma's boys!

THE SETBACK IS NOT THE END OF THE STORY PUSH YOURSELF TO YOUR NEXT GREAT CHAPTER

For the next few years, I lived in low-income housing while raising my boys and working at Woodward's department store. Then, I left my job at Woodward's and began a career in banking. I started out on the front lines working as a teller. After six weeks I was promoted to the prestigious side counter position. Within a year I was promoted again to managing tens of millions of dollars of lawyers' trust funds in an exclusive, independent position.

I was always pushing myself to be better, to do more, be more, have more so I could give more. I wanted to improve myself and my income to support my family. I had an internal drive to never give up. I wanted to prove everyone wrong. I would make it. I could do this! During these years I learned to appreciate life's lessons and gifts and I continued to grow.

Ten years after my first marriage, I married a second time. I became pregnant soon after our wedding in Hawaii but spent most of my time during our marriage being neglected by my husband. As soon as my daughter was born, I no longer existed in his eyes. I later found out that my husband had a girlfriend before, during, and after our entire marriage. He worked with her; she was married, too, and the four of us occasionally hung out together as couples. Needless to say, the marriage did not last, but I would not change a thing as I have my beautiful daughter from that relationship.

I spent the next years relentlessly trying to find my passion. I worked in banking, direct sales, office supplies, a genealogical search company, and as a sales manager for a roofing distribution company. I also went to night school while working full-time and raising my kids, to get my diploma in International Trade. Additionally, I began a calling card company in Santiago, Chile that I launched at the Canada/Chile Trade Mission in 2003.

OPPORTUNITY KEEPS KNOCKING, SO OPEN THE DOOR!

I was very proud of the calling card company. It was a crazy dream, but I wanted to make it happen. Recognizing a huge opportunity, I wanted to offer an affordable service that we took for granted in Canada. The large telecommunications companies had a very different view on my entry to the marketplace and I was forced out of business when they pressured my distribution channel to drop me. Unfortunately, my venture was short-lived after significant effort and money had been invested. I planned to travel back to Chile to negotiate a deal with another distributor when I was rear-ended in a car accident and suffered severe whiplash, leaving me unable to travel. I had to move on from this company but by this time I knew it was not the end. I knew other opportunities would come my way.

By 2007, I was working for a computer company selling proprietary software and hardware for restaurants. My expertise in sales and customer service had grown significantly by then. I had come a long way from the introverted little Greek girl who thought she was not good enough. With perseverance, training, and a belief in myself I had become a great salesperson.

I loved working with customers and was enjoying my new career when I began having severe migraines regularly. I was also having issues with my sinuses. I thought I probably had a severe sinus infection, but my nose and upper gums were numb, which was troubling.

That August was one big headache, literally. I had eight migraines that month and each one put me down for two to five days. I went to the doctor and had several tests run, including a CT scan. After the CT scan doctors finally determined the cause of my sinus trouble and migraines.

I will never forget that day. The doctor's office called and scheduled me for a 7:00 PM appointment. The doctor came in and told me that I had a brain tumor and that she was very sorry, but she did not know whether it was benign or malignant. She had not consulted a neurologist before meeting with me. I drove home in a state of shock and called my mom to tell her the news.

I learned that I had a meningioma, a benign brain tumor. After an MRI, I learned it measured 3.3 x 3.4 x 4.4 cm, was in my right frontal lobe, and had probably been growing for twenty or thirty years. Only recently had it grown large enough to begin causing migraines, sinus pain, and facial numbness.

Within a month I would be having major brain surgery to remove the tumor. Oddly enough, I was not scared until the day of the surgery, when it really sunk in. I had been told that the tumor was in an excellent location for surgery and that I would not need chemo or radiation afterwards. The tumor was not going to kill me. But with any surgery there is always a risk.

I do not remember much that happened the first week or so post-surgery. When I really came around and began noticing things, the first thing that caught my attention was that I was having significant vision problems. The brain surgeon had touched a nerve in my right eye, causing fourth nerve palsy. I always had this weird talent to do crazy thing with my eyes and move them independently, but this was something I could not control. I had severe double vision. I could only see straight when I looked through a very narrow view if I tilted my chin down. And I could not look to my left at all. When I tried, I lost all focus and control of my eyes.

This condition is similar to a child having a wandering eye. Actually, I had to be seen at Vancouver Children's Hospital to have my condition monitored. This was a very challenging time for me. It was one of the worst times of my life. I had so much stress and anxiety wondering if my vision would be like this forever. My head was permanently disfigured, leaving my self-esteem at an all-time low. My jaw was so stiff from surgery that I could barely open my mouth to eat. I was house-bound, and unable to walk up or down stairs without assistance. I could not read or watch TV to occupy myself because I was constantly dizzy. Every negative thought you could possibly imagine ran through my mind thousands of times each day. I wish I had known then what I know now about keeping a positive mindset, the healing powers of affirmations, an attitude of gratitude, and the law of attraction.

I cannot stress enough how important it is to reach out to family and friends to help you during a medical crisis (or any crisis, for that matter). Having people who love you to support you is so important. Being the independent person that I am, I did not ask for much help. Silly me. Stupid me, actually. I did not want to worry my kids any more than they already were. My mother was such an angel. She lived nearby and prepared meals for us, but for the most part, I was alone in my thoughts in a very dark place.

About five weeks into my recovery, I met someone online. Bored out of my mind, I had gone on a dating site, half-blind, looking for strangers to converse with me. Talk about being desperate! For our first meeting, I rode the bus to downtown Vancouver where we met for a drink. He must have thought I was rather forward on a first date when I grabbed his arm to walk up a few stairs. Little did he know that I grabbed his arm so that I would not fall flat on my face.

We hit it off and developed a relationship. He picked me up every day for several weeks and took me out on his random errands just to get me out of the house. Sometimes we would just hang out. At first, I only told him that I'd had a recent eye surgery. Eventually I told him the extent of the surgery. He was also having some challenges in his life, so it was wonderful to be able to help each other. I cannot tell you what a godsend he was for me. He came into my life exactly when I needed him, and I am forever grateful for what he did for me.

Worried about losing my job, I returned to work twelve weeks post-surgery. I was worried about paying my bills and the mortgage on the house I had recently purchased. I needed the money, or so I thought. In hindsight, that was the worst decision I could have made. I suffered with migraines and vision issues for several weeks before the universe decided I'd had enough. All of the senior managers, including me, were laid off from our jobs. It was the biggest blessing.

I did not work for two years. It was a very trying time. The line of credit was on a steady increase as the months went by, but I needed to heal. My vision took over a year to somewhat normalize, and the severe numbness in my face post surgery lasted for several years.

During this period, I had a lot of time to think. My surgery was a life-changing experience. I could have died. I decided to take on a totally different view on life from this time forward. From this point on, any time an opportunity presented itself I was going to take it.

DEFINE YOUR WORK AND WHAT YOU NEED

Knowing that after all my health problems I would need a job that allowed me to make my health a priority, I decided to choose a job that would work for me rather than choosing to work for the job. I started slowly by taking a 100% sales commission, part-time position that allowed me to work as much or as little as I wanted.

I told my bosses about my medical condition, and that I was not sure how I would respond to being back to work. My boss told me that as long as I was meeting or exceeding my quotas that he would not micromanage me. I would be allowed to do my own thing, which was perfect for me. For some this would be a scary venture to undertake, but I was up for the challenge.

I pushed myself by working long hours, often answering customer emails at 6:00 AM before I went to work and again well into the evening. I needed to build up my customer base and wanted to ensure they were well taken care of. Within less than six months I was working full-time and making a full-time income. I was back!

After working for this company for about four years, a couple of millennials were hired into the mix, and that changed everything for me. I was working independently with little interaction with my bosses for the most part and the millennials were cc'ing him on every email they sent. This is when my interest in generational differences in the workplace was first piqued.

Although I enjoyed the work and my co-workers, my bosses were a different story. My work environment left much to be desired. Receiving year-end bonuses based on sales is a standard practice in the world of sales. When I did not receive a bonus at the end of 2013 because my boss said I was "already making too much money," I decided to look at other business opportunities. Forever the entrepreneur!

I continued working my sales job while seeking other opportunities. I joined an Australian direct sales company and quickly rose to the top of their company, becoming one of their top 20 earners out of 20,000 consultants. I had 1,700 consultants on my team and was the only director in North America. I earned free trips to Australia, Dubai, Aruba, Florence, Manchester, Dallas, and Los Angeles. I finally left my sales job in 2016 to pursue my new business venture full-time.

DREAM BIG AND HELP OTHERS DREAM TOO

I LOVED working with my team. Coaching and mentoring were my passion. In October 2016, I attended a One Day to Greatness seminar with Jack Canfield in Kamloops, BC. After a brief conversation with Jack, I decided to take his Train the Trainer course to become a certified Success Principles Trainer. The intention was to share this new knowledge with my team. I had found purpose and passion in supporting others to build successful teams. I felt fulfilled when I saw their self-esteem and confidence grow. They were conquering their fears and winning!

Unfortunately, I had to resign from the direct sales company in February 2017 when they started having issues with production and delivery. Later that year the company declared bankruptcy. I went through a lot of stress, anxiety, and loss of sleep. Panic attacks became the daily norm for me. I had known the CEO for over eighteen years and was completely in the dark about the state of the company. My team was upset and blaming me. I received a constant stream of Facebook messages and harassing emails. The downfall of the company was out of my control, so I had to bow out. But this was not my first time at the rodeo. I knew that my story did not stop here if I chose to keep trying.

I met someone in late 2016 who introduced me to an opportunity to speak and train businesses on generational differences in the workplace. I was fascinated by this as I saw the struggles my own millennial children were having at work. I look back now at the communication challenges that existed in my previous jobs and wish I knew then how the different generations think and process information. I wanted to more closely understand their environment and what I could do to help. It made perfect sense that bridging the generation gap would improve productivity, communication, collaboration, and make for a happier, more cohesive work environment.

I now know that the behaviors, attitudes, beliefs, experiences, and influences during an individual's formative years really shape who they are and how they behave in all areas of their lives. I was excited about my new-found knowledge, and planned to launch my speaking business by mid-2017.

I hired an image consultant to come to my home and do a complete wardrobe change to prepare me for my speaking career. Having someone go through my wardrobe and tell me to get rid of most of it was a very difficult experience. There were a few tears. I must have attachment issues! I eventually embraced the change and spent thousands of dollars on a new wardrobe to complete my new look.

Then, as luck would have it, I broke a veneer on my front tooth. No big deal, I thought. I had been through this before and would just have it replaced.

This was the beginning of my dental nightmare. From May 31, 2017 through December 21, 2017, I had twenty-six dental appointments to fix my front tooth. I began lisping and developed what doctors believe is a stress-related condition. I lost the saliva in my mouth, had burning in my throat from acid reflux brought on by stress, my voice was constantly hoarse, and I spent several months waking up with panic attacks. I never knew from one to day to the next if I would have a voice or not, so I had to put everything on hold.

I saw every doctor and specialist I believed might be able to help me. I was taking six pills a day to help with my various symptoms. I hated this! I needed to feel better; I needed to heal my body naturally. I would not stop until I got the answers I needed. I moved away from traditional medicine, stopped taking all my medications, and began incorporating EFT (Emotional Freedom Technique), also known as Tapping, Reiki, and Bioenergy work, to heal my body.

Eventually, my body and voice were getting to the point where I could speak relatively well, I decided to move forward with the training business. I hired a business coach to get me on the right track, mentally and physically. He helped me tremendously during a very difficult time. I also attended Raymond Aaron's Speaker and Communication Workshop, which totally changed my training and speaking style. It gave me the confidence I was lacking and sent me on a whole new trajectory for my business. I began my own company, Gen-Connect Training in early 2018. It has been an amazing ride. I am much more at peace and ready for the next stage in my life.

LIVING IN THE POSITIVE HAS MADE MY LIFE

Although I have been blessed with many struggles, I have also enjoyed many successes. I have experienced relationships that did not work out, work and business challenges, worries when raising three children as a single parent, medical challenges, and many dreams and goals that seemed impossible. The one thing I always knew for sure was that if I gave up and wallowed in self-pity, I would be letting myself and my children down. That was not an option. Success was the only acceptable outcome.

I wanted to show my children what a strong, self-sufficient and resourceful mother I could be, and that they could always rely on me. I wanted to set an example and prove to myself and my children that I could provide for us no matter what. I am very proud of the amazing people my children have become; they are strong, independent, kind, respectful, and loving. This is the true meaning of success for me. Out of all the things I have accomplished thus far, they are my crowning glory.

FIVE STRATEGIES FOR A SUCCESSFUL LIFE

1) **Always have a positive mindset.** This is a crucial component. Before you get into the power of a positive mindset and the law of attraction, spend some time listening to what you are currently telling yourself. Check in with yourself. What is going on with you? We constantly speak to ourselves with an inner voice which is sometimes quietly whispering and sometimes yelling. Once you have spent a few days noticing how you speak to yourself, you may not like it very much; after all, you are your own worst critic. Be accountable for how you speak to yourself. Never fear, you have the power to change that inner voice!

Do you believe you are the product of everything that has happened to you in your life? Your inner voice may try to convince you that you are a victim of your circumstances and your past. Reflect and acknowledge the things that have happened to you and where you are now. Then prepare to move past them.

2) Shift your mindset using the law of attraction. You can influence things around you so that things happen FOR you rather than TO you. The universal principle of the law of attraction is that 'like attracts like.' The law of attraction manifests through your thoughts by drawing to you not only thoughts and ideas that are alike, but also people who think like you, along with corresponding situations and possibilities. It is the magnetic power of the universe which draws similar energies to each other.

The law of attraction is already working in your life, intentional or not. If you have a negative mindset, many unpleasant or unwanted things are probably happening in your life, and you may see negative things happening all around you. Think back to how you speak to yourself. Be mindful of your thoughts and that inner voice. Begin to think positively.

Along with thinking positively, begin to intentionally think and feel the things that you would like to have in your life. The most common things people desire are love, a career, good relationships, health, and wealth. Visualize a mental image of what you want to achieve. Repeat positive, affirming statements to create and bring into your life what you visualize or repeat in your mind. In other words, use the power of your thoughts and words.

Imagine that what you desire is already a part of your life. Acknowledge it with each of your five senses, to the extent that you can. Spend time imagining your life once you have acquired what it is that you want. Write out your affirmations and read them aloud at least once daily. You will begin to draw them to you when you act as though you already have what it is that you want. Persistence is key!

3) Take calculated risks. Do you encourage yourself to stay where you are and play it safe? Safe can be dangerous. I encourage you to take calculated risks. If you do not try new things you will never know how far you can go. When opportunities present themselves, jump on them. It may be your one and only chance. Push yourself and do not take no for an answer. Keep digging until you find the answer you want.

Quitting is always an option. Well, it is an option for those who are content living a mediocre life. Quitting is an option unless you want to live an amazing life with a purpose. If you want to live the life of your dreams, you must not give up. Do not give up and never stop learning. If you continue to learn, you will continue to grow both personally and professionally.

4) Appreciate all of life's lessons and gifts with an attitude of gratitude. Learn and grow from your failures. Let life's challenges teach you to persevere even when all you want to do is give up. Remind yourself that the only outcome you will accept is success.

5) NEVER Give Up. We all face adversities and challenges in life. It takes character, drive, and a positive mindset to persevere, overcome, and excel in life. The only person who can stop you from achieving your goals is you. If I can do it, so can you. Go for it!

Do you, your team, or organization want to be inspired to change your future and find your purpose?

Do you want to learn how mastering the Five Strategies for A Successful Life can empower you in both your personal and professional career?

Do you want to say "NO TO THE PITY PARTY" and achieve the life you truly desire?

Vivian Stark is an inspirational speaker and corporate trainer living in Vancouver, B.C. Canada, whose captivating story will inspire you to live the life you want if you never, never, never give up on what's important – You.

As a generational and workplace effectiveness expert, Vivian's career centers around helping others work in a more collaborative and cohesive work environment. Her focus on engagement and accountability both in and outside of the workplace mirrors her personal belief of how you must take 100% responsibility in all areas of your life. Learn how giving up blaming, complaining and excuse making can lead you to live a life filled with peace, happiness and personal fulfillment.

To learn how you can incorporate her knowledge and expertise into your life and business with ease and confidence, reach out to Vivian at www.gen-connect.ca. Vivian is available for private or corporate speaking engagements.

What Does Change Mean to You?

Fundamental Elements for a Vibrant, Fulfilling Life

TONY DEBOGORSKI

How do you view change? For many individuals, change has become something to fear. It invokes feelings of anxiety and potential loss. There is often little focus on what we can gain from change. Instead, the negative feelings and thought patterns overwhelm us, which can make change more difficult to accept and benefit from.

Think of the flight or fight response. Change, if we don't manage it effectively, can trigger that response. It can make us respond as if our lives are being threatened, when it's more likely that we are simply being affected by changing circumstances. Some of these circumstances are in our control and others are out of our control. However, if we can alter our reaction to change, then we can reap some amazing benefits.

Yes, you can benefit from change. However, in order to do so you need to be willing to create a new mindset in regards to how you view change and how you choose to act. Without the right mindset, you might be missing out on a change that could give depth to your life and the lives of those around you.

Changes, both those that happen to us and the ones that we create ourselves, have the potential to create new opportunities and experiences we might otherwise miss. These can give us another perspective and enrich our lives. Change did just that for me as a young man.

I grew up in rural Canada, where hard work and sweat were the building blocks of your success. I learned to be a jack of all trades, because that was the way you got things done around a farm. When I left to attend university, the idea was that I would end up coming home, marrying my high school girlfriend, and raising my family in the farming community where I was raised.

This step towards a university education was already a big change, since only a few of my family members actually went on to get a university education. Working hard was our way of life, and it was hard physical work. I couldn't imagine any other way, but university gave me a new way to live and introduced me to the idea of working smarter, not harder.

My life was enriched by not only the classes I attended, but the people I met. I was exposed to those who hadn't lived their entire life on a farm.

I was exposed to different perspectives on how to tackle a variety of challenges. It altered my perception of the world, giving me a broader viewpoint. At the same time, I also deepened my appreciation of the values my parents instilled in me.

It was my first experience with change, but definitely not my last. I took the step to open my mind to change, which allowed me to get comfortable with the idea. During this time, I learned that it was okay to find assistance in accepting a change and acting on it without fear. The life I live today is defined by change. Now, instead of fear and anxiety, I welcome change for the blessings it may bring. How did I get to this point? It started with my willingness to learn and grew from there.

There is a process to change, but if we are not careful, we can actually prolong the process and make it more difficult. Let's walk through the reality of change. First, you have the old status quo. This is the reality of how things are right now. It could be a fairly peaceful way of life or you could find it difficult, but it is what you know.

Now a foreign element is introduced. It could be a new job or a move, for example. Most of the time, our first reaction is to resist, fearing the chaos that we are sure is to follow. After a point, we see the transforming idea of change and begin to integrate it into our lives. As time goes on, we then integrate the change into our lives and thus create a new status quo. Still, the impact of many aspects of this process can be lessened if we take a different point of view toward change.

Through mentors and my own experiences, I learned the key elements that can impact your ability to not only weather change, but thrive in the process. These five key elements are necessary to create the right mindset, one that embraces change, instead of being governed by a fear of change.

KEY #1. SELF-BELIEF

The first key is your belief in yourself. This is the foundation of a vibrant and fulfilling life. Without confidence in your own ability to handle challenges, you will see change as a crisis, instead of a benefit or an opportunity to grow as an individual.

Throughout our lives, we are told how to act, dress, and even think. Our belief systems are influenced by this training. In addition, as we grow older and other influences come into play from the world around us. Just take a moment and think about all the people and ideas you encounter on a daily basis. These could be teachers, family members, workmates, television, the internet, etc. The list goes on and on.

All of these influences are not focused on teaching us to think for ourselves, but instead are focused on developing our thinking to fall in line with who they believe we should be. Call it the social conditioning of our world. There often isn't time to learn who we are, to spend time with ourselves, to think, imagine, and explore the world. Instead, if we don't buy out the time, we can find that we are dissatisfied with our lives and unable to determine why.

We often have our purpose in life defined for us by others. This can lead to a lack of fulfillment in our lives, especially if what we are supposed to be doesn't fit our true vision of who we are.

The key is to stop and examine your belief system. Focus on your values. How many of them would you say you genuinely believe and how many have you taken on because of someone else in your life? It is amazing how many of our beliefs may no longer be serving us, but we are still using them to define ourselves and the world around us. Like the traditional fall and spring cleaning of our homes, we need to constantly be willing to clean the beliefs that no longer serve us or contribute to the growth and happiness of our lives from our consciousness.

Do you wake up in the morning satisfied with where you are in life? Can you look in the mirror and see a face excited to meet the day? Do you feel accountable for your life or does it feel as if your life is happening to you? How you see the world is based on your self-belief. What crafts your self-belief?

It hinges on your ability to see yourself master a skill and then be able to do it again and again successfully. Positive experiences help us grow our confidence in ourselves and define who we are. These moments often start in our early childhood, setting up a pattern throughout our lives.

My first memory of confidence building occurred when I was 11 years old. The regional elementary track and field meet was coming up. I wanted to win the top male athlete award. Although I had participated in the meet in the past, I hadn't won before. This time, I decided to do things differently. In preparation for the meet, I spent extra time training, including running after school. I was determined and my goal dominated my thoughts. It was a type of visualization, one that helped build my confidence going into the meet.

I had entered into five events and there were points for coming into first, second, and third place. On the day of the meet, it was sunny, the field and track were dry. Conditions were perfect for this outdoor event. My focus was on doing my best to earn the most points possible. At the end of the event, I had four first place ribbons and one for second place. I was presented with the trophy for top male athlete. That feeling of accomplishment boosted my sense of what I could do and built my self-belief.

What goals have you set that you were able to accomplish on your own? How did you feel after you achieved your goal? Setting and accomplishing goals is a great way to feel better about yourself. How does this translate into having a different mindset about change? When you feel confidence in your abilities, you will not find yourself fearing change and the challenges it can present.

However, in the midst of a major change, you might find yourself neglecting your needs. How often do we put ourselves last when others around us are in need of our time and attention? While we might think that it will last for only a short period of time, putting ourselves on the back burner can become a routine, one that has a negative impact on our lives.

This can leave you worn out mentally and put you into a negative frame of mind. I can point to research and personal experiences to give you examples of why a negative mindset can be the anti-change and can encourage you to avoid thinking about the potential benefits of change. Once you focus on caring for your needs, you are in a better position to weather change and give assistance to others. Once you find confidence and strength in yourself and your abilities, you will be able to master whatever change and challenges come your way.

One important point is that you might still be afraid, but don't let it paralyze you into not acting at all. Remember those moments of success and allow them to motivate you to keep going. The keys to being self-reliant are perseverance, dedication, and integrity. When you have them, you will be able to conquer just about anything.

KEY #2. PURPOSE

Your life is a journey and you are the navigator. Some individuals choose to navigate based on their surroundings, essentially letting the waves aimlessly lead them along. In the end, that kind of life rarely leads to happiness with change or with yourself. You become a product of your circumstances, instead of defining yourself on your own terms.

What is purpose? According to the American Heritage Dictionary, it is "The object toward which one strives or for which something exists, an aim or a goal. The reason for which anything is done, created or exists, an aim or a goal."

When you examine your own life, are you excited about what you do? Could you define the purpose of your life? For some, their purpose becomes apparent when they are young. They find the passion that defines their lives and shapes their careers. Others never find that purpose, leaving them to struggle to find satisfaction with their lives.

If you haven't defined the purpose of your life, then it is time to think about what you enjoy. What sparks your passion? What gets you excited to get out of bed in the morning? Once you start to define your purpose, set your goals around what you enjoy. This can help you gain perspective on your purpose.

However, keep in mind that your purpose is not set in stone. It can change over time as you gain life experience and a better understanding of yourself. Taking action will help you be drawn to what you like. Try new things. Consider the spiritual influences in your life. To postulate is the act of creation. It can happen when you think, write, or speak something into being. Focus, because if you think it, then you can do it.

Change can be initiated by you. It doesn't have to be dominated by circumstances outside of your control. You can start by taking one action that will move you closer to a specific goal. That goal could be to simply change your way of thinking or to release a belief that is no longer serving you, but could be limiting you instead.

With your purpose defined, you could move forward to produce the life you want and mindset for change, which starts with how you take care of yourself.

KEY #3. HEALTH

Fear and anxiety can have physical repercussions. They impact how our bodies feel, as well as our ability to fight off illnesses and deal with chronic conditions. Research has proven time and again that our minds can influence our physical well-being.

Are you poisoning your body through the negative thoughts you are dwelling on? To create the energy necessary for a vibrant fulfilling life you need to maximize your mental state, maintain your physical body, and nourish yourself properly. Keep your mind focused on what is possible, instead of focusing on what can't be done or any potentially negative consequences.

The combination of your mind and body is a synergistic relationship. It means you need to take care of both to achieve overall well-being. To start, let's focus on your physical body. Are you getting out on a regular basis to exercise and stretch your muscles? Do you raise your heart rate? One of the interesting side effects of physical activity is how it can impact our mood. When we are uplifted in mood, it translates into our thought processes. Regular physical exercise can contribute to greater overall positivity in our lives.

If you find it hard to get out on your own and get physically active, then consider finding a support group, a partner, or even a gym where you can be held accountable for showing up and putting in the effort. You will appreciate the results in terms of your health, making it worth the effort. Additionally, the physical benefits will allow you to grow in other areas of your life, thus making change more welcome, especially as your body grows stronger.

When it comes to your physical well-being, the reality is that you are what you put into your body. If you don't fuel your body for optimal performance, then it can't give you the very best physically. That can have a domino effect on how you operate mentally. When you are tired and not feeling your best, can you honestly say that you have made your best decisions? Or do you find yourself rethinking those choices at a later date?

There are five products, which I refer to as the five white poisons, that you need to be aware of. They can be found in a variety of foods throughout your local grocery store. So much of what we eat today has been processed extensively, removing the natural nutrients and fiber-rich parts. As a result, we are exposed to more of these five products than ever before. What are these five white poisons? Sugar, starch, flour, salt, and milk.

All of these are foods that need to be consumed in moderation. Recognize that they are often hidden ingredients within other foods. Therefore, it is wise to limit your intake wherever possible to make sure you aren't putting too much of these items into your body.

Part of your physical health is also caring for your brain. Think of it as a muscle. Like every muscle in your body, it is important to allow it to relax and get the necessary rest. This can be done through meditation or even finding some quiet time away from your family and friends to relax and think quietly without distraction. Doing so also allows you to reduce your stress level. Making sure your stress level comes down will positively impact your mental health as well.

Do you have a place that brings you peace? Having this place allows you to mentally unwind and just let go of your stress, even if it is just temporarily. Meditation is a method that you can use, even if all you can do is go to a quiet place in your home or office. There are a variety of meditation techniques available. Some individuals prefer a calming form of music to accompany their meditation, while others prefer to just enjoy the silence. Whatever you prefer, the point is to make your mental health a priority. If you do, it will be much easier to handle change and thrive.

Change can bring benefits and give us opportunities we might not otherwise have considered without the upheaval in our lives. But in order to benefit from change, we need to maintain our positivity, both physically and mentally. This can be hard to do when a change has a particularly emotional impact. Relying on family and friends for support is key to dealing with the more emotional aspects of any change in your life.

Throughout this discussion of your health, I haven't really touched on one area that impacts our well-being. That is our relationships. But how do they impact our lives and what do we need to remember about these relationships when it comes to change?

KEY #4. RELATIONSHIPS

Did you know that you are shaped by the people you spend the most time with? Those individuals will influence your ideas, beliefs, and actions. This also extends to your attitude. If you are surrounded by positive thinkers, it is much easier to maintain a positive attitude. Think about the last time you were surrounded by negative individuals. After a while, did it seem as if that negative and critical spirit rubbed off on you?

Here are some questions to ask yourself about the people you spend time with. Are they primarily positive or negative? Do you find yourself having spirited conversations with plenty of give and take, or do you find that you are just a dumping ground for all their complaints about life?

If you want to create change in your life or be more accepting of the changes in your life, then you may need to assess who you spend most of your time with. Creating a new attitude or shifting your thought process means assessing who is influencing them both and whether that influence is helping or hurting.

When I was finishing my university education, I was associating with a group of friends who were eager to join the corporate world. I had worked in the corporate world during my summer breaks, but I had also started a business installing sprinkler systems in areas where there was new home construction. I did this after hours and on weekends. Although I was working a lot, I was also figuring out that I didn't have to go the corporate route to be successful. My small part-time business had made me more money than my daily corporate job.

Our final year of school came and, of course, my friends and I discussed what our next steps were as we started life after university. Some had mixed feelings about what direction to take after graduating. The options included attempting to open a business in the role of entrepreneur or applying to one of the many companies out there for a traditional corporate role.

Since most of my friends decided to go the corporate route, I did too, even though my experience indicated that I could be equally, if not more, successful in the role of entrepreneur. The individuals I associated with provided acknowledgement and support during that decision-making period of my life.

Are there some decisions where you can see the influence of your associates? Can you look back now and see that perhaps a different decision would have been more appropriate for the path you ultimately wanted to pursue?

While we all want to think that we are independent thinkers, sudden influences from our associates can impact what we choose to do and how we think and act. Yet, with a greater understanding of who you are as a person (your goals and your passions), you will find that you can truly be an independent thinker and identify the effect of those influences around you.

Self-knowledge takes time, but the reward is a better way to embrace life and the change around us, both personally and professionally. If you want to move down a specific path toward your goal, you need to make sure to associate with like-minded individuals. They can encourage and support you as you work to achieve those specific milestones.

As you discover what you are passionate about, you will be able to find like-minded friends and associates who are focused on that particular activity or pursuit. For instance, you may be passionate about helping young people. There may be local groups geared toward providing activities and mentorship to teenagers within your community. Getting involved in those groups will put you around others who share your passion, which can help motivate you even further.

Take the time to examine your beliefs and determine if the friends you are associating with are the right people to support you in the next stage or season of your life. Not everyone you spend time with will be an active part of helping you achieve your goals. However, they can be the individuals who make you laugh, as well as help you see the positive when situations or circumstances seem overwhelming.

The point is to be around people who embrace change and can help you to do the same. When it comes to your mindset, negative association will eventually bring even the most positive mindset down. Have you ever tried to accomplish something that you had already decided was impossible? It becomes an uphill battle, and you likely didn't succeed.

A positive attitude, on the other hand, makes it possible for you to achieve even more than you thought was possible. In addition, your positive mindset could have an influence on those around you. Imagine being a positive influence to those who are important to you. The best relationships are the ones where you both are actively working to support and encourage each other in pursuit of your passions, while being there for each other during times of major change or upheaval that life seems to throw at us all.

If you are looking to make adjustments to your circle of friends and associates, consider looking into your community for opportunities to meet new people. Some ideas include joining a club or charity organization. If there is an activity that you have been interested in trying, why not sign up for lessons? What things have you been afraid to try for one reason or another? Why not give one of those things a try? If your fear is that you won't do well, make peace with that and do it anyway. You might find that as you conquer your fear, you make new friends that will enrich your life.

I want to point out here that the idea is to make you better able to adapt to change and train yourself to see the benefit of change versus focusing on the fear and anxiety. Each of these new experiences is putting you in charge of creating change in your life on a smaller scale, which will make it easier for you to handle change on a larger scale.

The most rewarding sport even for me was signing up and participating in triathlons. I was a prairie boy who didn't grow up around water. Signing up for a triathlon forced me to learn how to swim. I could have let fear of the unknown stop me, but instead I broadened my horizons.

Additionally, I signed up with a friend. We challenged each other and held each other accountable for attaining our goals. It was not an easy journey, but I found new strength as I pushed myself and supported my friend.

The 10-month journey before my first triathlon was grueling at times. It included swim lessons, getting the proper equipment, the proper bike, the right shoes, and more. After those 10 months of training, lessons, and standing up to my own fears, the day of the race finally came.

The first leg of the triathlon was swimming, which I can definitely say was not my strength. In fact, when I ran into the water, I was with a pack of men, but after a few minutes of kicking and banging around, I was alone and about ready to give up. Instead of doing that, I pulled back for a moment, composed myself, and then started to swim, concentrating on one stroke at a time.

I finished dead last in the swim, but at least I finished. I continued with ease to do the bike and run, completing those two legs in top times. I was dead last overall, because of my slow swim, but I still felt a great sense of accomplishment because I had completed my goal. In the process, I had met many new people who shared an interest in triathlons. I also got closer to my friend Nick, who trained with me and completed the same triathlon.

It was a rewarding event for me, not only because I actually finished what

I set out to do, but because when I went out to celebrate that night, I met my future wife. Our relationship has been full of change and challenges, but none of the joys would have been possible if I hadn't stepped outside of my comfort zone to try something new and conquered a fear at the same time.

Think about the various relationships in your life. Could there be someone who is already in your life who would be supportive as you step outside your comfort zone? Those individuals are the ones who will support you through change. They are key relationships to nurture. Still, those relationships will not be able to support you if you are not able to communicate your needs to those critical people in your life. As a result, my fifth key is also the most critical: communication.

KEY #5. COMMUNICATION

No matter who we are and what we do throughout the day, we are constantly communicating. We use our faces, our hands, and, of course, our speech to communicate what we are thinking and feeling on a daily basis.

Yet within the realm of communication, the opportunities for misunderstandings abound. There are literally hundreds of thousands of examples throughout history demonstrating how misunderstandings can grow into much larger breakdowns of relationships between individuals, groups, and even countries.

Communication is truly an incredible concept. Great communicators can wow us and bring difficult concepts or ideas into focus. Have you ever heard the speeches of Martin Luther King Jr.? Decades after his passing, his words continue to move people. Then there are more current examples, such as Tony Robbins, Bob Proctor, or Brian Tracy. All of these individuals are amazing in their delivery of self-help information. Listen to their presentations and you can see how they really connect with their audiences.

Change requires communication, but change doesn't go over well if it is not communicated well. Every parent who communicates with a teenager can appreciate this point. Their child may not be able to articulate their frustration or the reasons behind it. An argument often becomes par for the course, leaving everyone frustrated and out of sorts. Misunderstandings can make change difficult to handle, because you may not understand why the change is occurring.

Companies often make this mistake as well. They may not clearly communicate their vision, so when they make changes, their employees are often left feeling frustrated and out of the loop. It can also make them feel uncertain about their job security, which can negatively impact their productivity. The reality is that miscommunication can have a large impact on whether change is welcomed or feared.

Communication is more than just speaking clearly. It is listening to and understanding the concerns of the other person and doing your best to address those concerns. When it comes to creating change in your life, you may find that you need to explain to your family why you are making that change. How do you communicate your choice? Often, how well it is communicated is reflected in the level of support you receive and if the change is embraced or not.

Have you been part of a change where the communication was less than you expected? How did that impact your ability to accept the change and create something incredible from that opportunity? For many of us, the answer is that the change was more difficult and we likely didn't support it wholeheartedly.

Again, the point is that communication can make a change easier to accept or a lack of it can make the implementation of a change more difficult. If you are initiating change in your own life, be sure that you are clearly communicating your needs to those around you. While they may not always agree with your decisions, they are much more likely to support them and the changes you want to make if you can clearly communicate the change and its impact.

Along with good communication, you need to be a good listener. Often misunderstandings occur because one individual is not really listening to the other. They may miss key instructions or details that could make the situation clearer. As a result, it can be easy to act without truly knowing all the necessary facts and circumstances. Can you see how not listening well could impact how you feel about a change in your life? It is also easy to see how others might be less supportive of change you initiate if they weren't listening.

How can you tell if someone is truly hearing you? Ask them questions and then clarify when it appears that they may not have gotten an accurate picture of what is about to occur. Some individuals may want to willfully misunderstand, and you want to do everything in your power to avoid that. At the same time, be a good listener. Don't listen to respond, but listen to understand their concerns, worries, and potential fears. Make adjustments to address their concerns where possible, but be as reassuring as you can when those adjustments might not be possible.

When you don't listen, you run the risk of missing key instructions or information that could directly impact your life or the change you are about to make.

I was always working, even from a young age. For a period of time, I worked on a gravel crusher as a ground person. My job was to go around and check for broken wheels, conveyors, and signs of wear and tear on other components. If something was wrong, I was to report it immediately to the tower person overseeing the operation. His job was to shut down the entire mechanical operation so the problem could be addressed. If he didn't, a major failure could occur, which could end up costing thousands of dollars of damage.

One morning, I was tired and didn't pay attention when I was relieving the previous shift. I had missed that a flashing was tearing and did not report it. An hour later, that flashing tore through. My boss saw it first. Gravel was everywhere. He had the operation stopped, then came over to the tool shack to fire me for not properly checking the system. That miscommunication cost the company time and money, plus I lost my job. The lesson? Communication and paying attention to the details is key to success in any area of your life, but especially when you are initiating major change.

Now let's talk about how a lack of communication can contribute to conflict. Our ability to connect with others can be hampered if we don't communicate well or if we are not sensitive to their needs and hot spots. Our personal and professional lives can be impacted by poor communication.

If you are considering acting to make changes in your life, start with how you communicate with others. We can all find areas to improve and make our connections with others deeper and more meaningful. The art of language is not easy. From birth, we are trained to communicate, but it doesn't come easily to all of us. Some become better than others at expressing themselves. The art of communication can be terrifying and amazing at the same time. You may also find it difficult to express yourself, especially when dealing with loved ones. How can you communicate more effectively with the individuals in your life?

Start by asking questions. This helps you gather information. Repeat back to the speaker your understanding of what they just said in response to your question. If they don't agree with your interpretation, keep asking for clarification until you get it. Be sure that you genuinely listen to the response before you start making assumptions. Try and imagine the situation from the other person's point of view. Be patient, because the best communication takes time.

There are also classes on public speaking and the art of communication. If you find yourself struggling consistently in this area, consider taking a course. The principles and real-world practice can help you improve your general communication skills. If you find yourself losing your train of thought, then consider writing down what you want to say. Be clear and concise where possible. Then use your written thoughts as a platform to bring up various points when appropriate within the context of the conversation.

Don't underestimate the power of practicing your communication skills in front of a mirror. This is where you can work on eye contact, exploring your various facial expressions, and also how to speak clearly. If you can talk to yourself, then it will get easier to talk to others. Make an effort to come out of your comfort zone, especially if you are not a good communicator. Consider it a change for the better.

Recognize that by improving your communication skills you can improve the quality of your life, as well as weather changing circumstances more effectively.

MOVE FORWARD WITH ME

Throughout this chapter, I have focused on some key areas that can make change more palatable, and reduce the fear and anxiety that commonly occurs. Still, the reality is that change, especially change we didn't initiate, can be overwhelming. Over the course of my lifetime, I have dealt with a variety of changes and I can say that not every experience was pleasant. But they all taught me valuable lessons.

I also want to remind you that change doesn't need to be something that occurs to you, but can be something you initiate. Consider areas of your life that are not as satisfying as you would like them to be. For example, are you struggling financially, but find yourself reluctant to make changes or take the risks necessary to turn your financial life around? Here is an area where making a change happen can have a significant impact.

However, don't limit yourself merely to material affluence. There are literally dozens of areas where you could find yourself hesitating to make changes. No matter what change you want to make, the mindset you choose will determine whether the change is successful or a struggle.

Throughout my work with individuals on changes in their lives, one thing has become clear; your mindset is key to making change work for you and allowing yourself to embrace change effectively.

I'm willing to work with you to help create the change that you want to see in your life. Let's face it, changes to our self-belief can lead to even more significant changes in other areas of our lives. With an improvement to your self-belief, there is no telling what you can accomplish. The changes to your point of view about yourself and what you can accomplish will help you make different choices about how you choose to live and work.

I believe that coaching is key to creating the right mindset to initiate and absorb changes in your life. A positive mindset allows you to see change in terms of what is possible, instead of focusing on the potential losses. Until you take the leap, you will never know exactly what is possible. But it can be hard to take those first steps to overhauling your thought process on your own.

I believe strongly in coaching and mentorship. It is a way to pass on the wisdom you have learned and the key strategies you may have discovered for addressing and initiating change. As part of my efforts to help others embrace change, my coaching and mentorship is available to you.

In my book, The Book of Change, I tackle a variety of topics and areas where you can start making small changes to build up to bigger ones. I also discuss how you can take dramatic and difficult circumstances and use them to learn and grow.

Using these tools, you can make a difference in your own life and in the lives of others. You can go from being fearful of change to being an example of embracing change for those in your family, your social circle, and your community. However, coaching isn't the only way to work on your skills to create and embrace change.

You can become a change advocate. That means allowing your positive mindset regarding change to influence others and impact their attitudes toward possible changes in their own lives. Your own example of dealing with change can serve as inspiration for others, which can then allow them to turn themselves into change advocates. It is a never ending cycle, which can give you peace of mind, even when faced with the toughest of challenges.

Additionally, there are other key takeaways for you to keep in mind as you start the journey to create change in your life. One way to embrace it is to understand what is happening and even to learn why.

Continuing education allows you to take the fear out of any change. After all, most of the fear of change stems from a lack of knowledge about what the change will mean for you, your family, and your community. When we are informed, change can be less intimidating, which can make us less fearful and more willing to take risks. Change is a part of taking risks to grow and explore our passions, achieve our goals, and fulfill our dreams. Without the right information and mindset, we will be unwilling to take the risks needed to achieve everything we imagine possible.

Clearly, you need to remember that change is a constant in your life. No one can escape it, no matter how risk adverse they may be. You need to embrace change for the benefits it can provide by creating a different mindset, gaining new skills, or even just acknowledging the personal growth that has resulted.

The change you see in your lifetime can and likely will have a profound impact on the lives of others, both now and in the future. Respect the people around you and demonstrate love and support when they are faced with changes, both large and small.

Contact me at **tony@tonydebogorski.com**. I would love to explore the ways that I can help you create real change in your life through adjustments to your mindset and increasing your willingness to learn and explore. Be inspired to create the meaningful life that you have always wanted and step away from living in fear of the unknown.

Amazing things are waiting for you! It is time for you to take the first step towards being a change agent in your own life.

Motivation Does Activate and Sustain Behaviour

How to Bring Results in Life and Business

JULIE HOGBIN

Before we talk about motivation in any great detail, it would be a good idea to cover the basics about what motivation really is. There are many, many, theories and huge amounts of research has been conducted on the subject over many decades. To be honest, with all the information out there it can be confusing as to what it all means.

One thing is for sure, one theory — one piece of information — does not cover it all as each researcher has their own bent and interpretation on the subject. It is when you are able to link it all together that it starts to make sense and you are able to do something with the information to help yourself.

I have researched, read about, practiced, and taught this subject to over 20,000 Leaders in Life, Business and the Entrepreneur market, both one-on-one and in small groups for very nearly three decades, and I am still learning.

This chapter is based around my knowledge, my interpretation, and a definition of Motivation that I have worked with for a long time. I have neither found nor developed a better definition — yet!

"Motivation is a conscious or unconscious driving force that arouses and directs action towards the achievement of a desired goal."

ClaimYourDestiny.global   #ConsciousLeadership

So, what does this mean in reality? It means that we are motivated by internal and external factors and that sometimes we know what those factors are and sometimes we don't: Our actions and thoughts are both conscious and unconscious in nature. It also means that the motives provoke a reaction and an action that help us 'get' something we want — a goal — and as a driving force they are powerful.

So my 1st questions to you are:

- What is your goal?

- What are you working towards?

- How many goals do you have?

- What is driving you?

- How conscious are you?

Motivation is an internal force; we are the only ones who can motivate us. Motivation can be affected by external influences. Ultimately it is us, and only us, that make the decision to do or not to do something. Nobody can make you feel or do anything! It is your absolute choice to capitulate and do, or to resist and not do.

We make the decision based on the information we have at the time and how confident we feel. There are many emotions and personal characteristics that come into play when we are talking about motivation and all that entails.

When we say that others motivate us what it really means is that they have created an environment that inspires us to do something. We make the decision out of fear in some cases, because we know it makes sense in other cases, because we aspire to be like the individual, or, more simply, just because we want to.

For you, and everybody else, your desired goal always provides you with a positive outcome. It gives you something you want even if that want is unconsciously driven. For others viewing it from their perspective, that outcome may be viewed as negative.

Let me explain what I mean with a couple of examples.

Addicts of any description do whatever it takes to fuel their need. They are achieving their desired outcome with more alcohol, more food, less food, more drugs, or just more of something, and they will go to extreme lengths to get it, such as selling personal and other people's belongings, lying and deceiving, going into debt and stealing.

Someone comes home with great intent of doing some research, maybe to write a book or to do some personal development such as going to the gym, and they end up sitting in front of the TV for hours with a bottle of wine. What is their driving force? We may not understand it as the viewer but there is definitely one for the person being observed.

Let's look at a couple of positive examples with a more generally accepted encouraging outcome.

A young person decides what they want to achieve in their life. They study like crazy to get the grades required to get to the top university and to study in a class of four with the top professor in their subject matter field, and they achieve it.

An individual from an underprivileged background wants to change their life, achieve greater things than have ever been achieved in their family, and become independently wealthy, and they are successful in achieving their goals.

Now for every example shared the opposite can be true as well. Not everybody becomes an addict, not everyone slouches in front of the TV, not every student achieves their potential, and not every underprivileged individual becomes independently wealthy.

"Everything you do is goal-driven. Everything you do is because you want the end result — whatever that end result may be!"

ClaimYourDestiny.global   #ConsciousLeadership

The examples are all based on how motivated the individual is to achieve their goal. Now if you know your goal consciously, can keep it in focus and resist the temptation of your old ways, you can achieve marvellous results.

The rest of this chapter will look at what drives you and how you can change your habits and behaviours over a period both short and long term, with the aim to achieve whatever it is you want.

I reference no theory in this chapter. There are many to read and learn which are of use to us all intellectually and unless the theory is practically applied and interpreted into reality all they remain are theories. I have spent decades interpreting theories into real life behaviours that make a difference for the better.

A few more questions for you to think about first.

- What are your drivers?

- What are your values?

- What is your risk tolerance?

- How much do you want to fit in with the 'norm' of your social group?

- How much do you really want, on a scale of 1 to 10, the thing it is you are aiming to achieve?

- How comfortable are you with change?

There are a lot more questions to ask but these will start you on the journey to understand your own motivators.

"Your motives create your habits, for good and bad, as they are your driving force."

ClaimYourDestiny.global #ConsciousLeadership

There is so much information coming at us on a minute by minute basis. We make thousands upon thousands of decisions every day — so many in fact, we cannot be conscious of all the decisions, to do or not to do something, that we do make. We would be completely overwhelmed if we did.

So what do we do? We create patterns of behaviour that we do not have to think about, as it is quicker that way, to achieve our outcomes. We create habits that get us what we want in the easiest manner.

"Your habits have created your behaviour through your values, beliefs, and attitudes."

ClaimYourDestiny.global #ConsciousLeadership

HABITS

Habits are a set of thoughts, behaviours, and ways of being that are developed through repeated behaviour. Habits are formed from the moment we become aware that there is a 'norm' of how to do things. Some we pick up from our parents, guardians, siblings, and influential individuals around us at a very early age. Others we develop for ourselves through the maturing process.

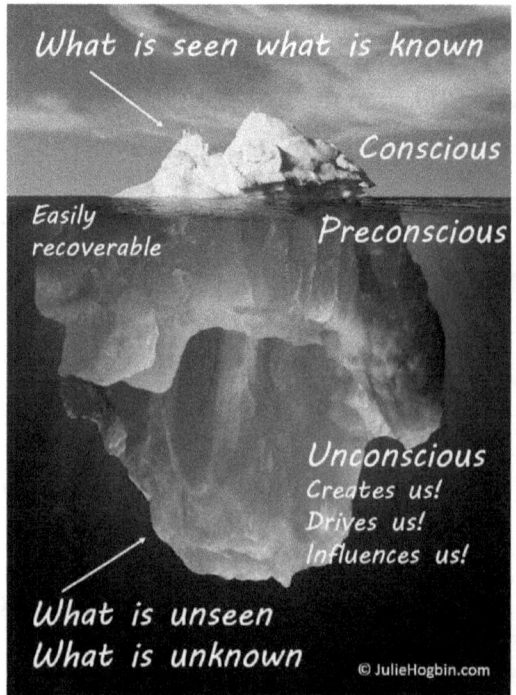

116

"Look to your parents for your beliefs about the world and yourself – you may be amazed at the similarities."

ClaimYourDestiny.global   #ConsciousLeadership

Once habits are created they can be difficult to break. To break a habit, we must consciously think about doing something different and then do it — which can equal hard work and being uncomfortable.

The thing is, we can all break habits if we really want to. BUT (and there is a big BUT) the unconscious part of our being is there to keep us safe. Any change and it may feel we are under threat and revert quickly to the old ways.

"Talk to your unconscious and ask its permission if you want to change some deep held habits and motivations to do things in a new way."

"Sounds a bit weird? Well it works, try it for yourself."

ClaimYourDestiny.global   #ConsciousLeadership

VALUES

Your values are a central part of who you are and who you want to be. By becoming more aware of these driving motivators in your life, you can use them as a guide to make the best choice in any situation.

Your decisions and actions, when in line with your values, will be easy to make and put into practice. If you are attempting to do something that is not held as a value to you, you will find it harder to do and, potentially, you will be in conflict with yourself.

Here is an example. If one of your values is honesty and you are in a relationship, business or personal, with someone who you know tells untruths, how hard will you find it to trust them? What will this do to your behaviour and your motivation within the relationship?

Values can be worked with, reordered, and installed — so do not lose hope. I personally have needed to work hard on my value regarding money. To say the least, it was slightly askew!

ATTITUDES

Your attitude is a predisposition to respond either negatively or positively towards an idea, object, person, or situation. It is the way you feel about something or someone. It can also be a particular feeling or opinion. It is seen as a conscious behaviour but will come from an unconscious driver.

Your attitude evolves as a result of your beliefs and values and will influence:

- Your choice of action and behaviour

- Your response to challenges

- Your response to incentives

- Your response to a word

- Your response to someone trying to help you

We all have an attitude — we cannot not have one. Generally, when it is said someone has an attitude it is meant as a negative opinion, but attitudes are drivers for good as well. It is just a common adaptation of a word which is more often linked to negativity.

As with anything else we do, our attitude is a choice we make. My choice, and I trust yours as you are reading this book, is to start each day with a positive attitude — it soon becomes a habit.

If you want to change something in your life, surround yourself with those who are on the same path or learn from those who have already done the 'thing' that you want to do. Attitudes are contagious so eradicate those personally held by yourself and those that are owned by people that may be in your circle who aren't helping you. If you don't know what your attitudes are, ask someone for feedback who will tell you the truth.

Also carefully study your close associates to make your own decisions on who stays with you on your journey and who leaves, their attitudes can be contagious. Look at the relationships that are in your life and acknowledge whether they are supporting you or hindering you. Decisions then can be made from a realistic position of what you want to do.

SOCIAL INTELLIGENCE

Social intelligence indicates that portions of our knowledge acquisition can be directly related to observing others within the context of social interactions, experiences and media influences.

So what does this mean to all of us? Basically, it means that if we see something that is rewarded, we copy it so that we get rewarded. We achieve the same result as we have observed, therefore we have achieved our result, which was our goal. There is far more to it but that's the basic concept. We learn by example from others.

So who do we copy? We copy those close to us and we adopt behaviours to fit into the crowd and belong. As we get older, we copy those who we admire or those who we aspire to be like. We develop a sense of self and become more aware of what it is we want. We begin to lead rather than follow — well some of us do and I expect you are a leader since you are reading this book! Join my Facebook group for more, https://www.facebook.com/groups/ClaimYourDestiny/

We are motivated to belong to a group with a certain set of characteristics. That could be because it is what we want or it can be because we know no different. It can be through peer pressure or choice, but whichever route we take it is ultimately our choice!

Join my Facebook group for more, https://www.facebook.com/groups/ClaimYourDestiny/

It is these drivers of behaviour that make you act differently from, or the same as, others in any given situation. So, by understanding these drivers, you can better understand why you do the things you do. The skill is not only to

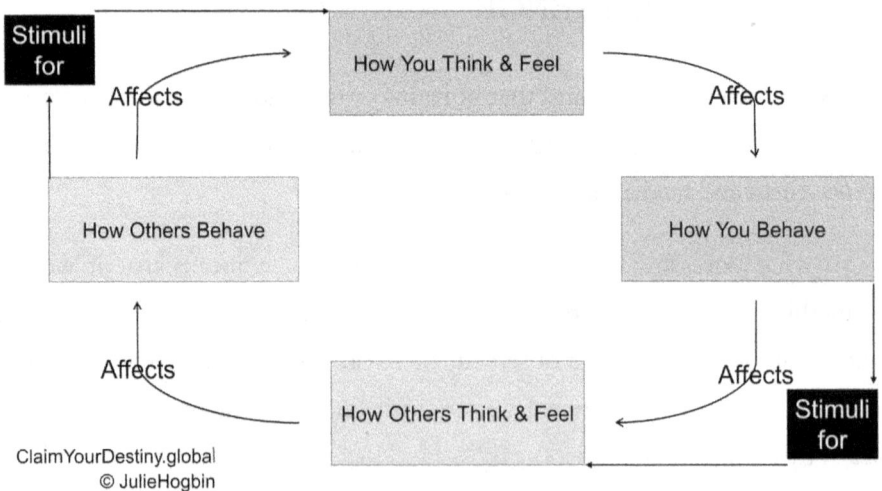

Stimuli for	Affects	How You Think & Feel	Affects
How Others Behave			How You Behave
Affects	How Others Think & Feel	Affects	Stimuli for

ClaimYourDestiny.global
© JulieHogbin

understand your conscious needs, but also those that are unconscious in nature.

"In the choice between changing one's mind and proving there's no need to do so, most people get busy on the proof."

– John Kenneth Galbraith

SELF-PERCEPTION

Self-perception is the belief or disbelief in our own capabilities to achieve a goal or an outcome. These beliefs provide the foundation for human motivation, well-being, and personal accomplishment. This is because unless you believe that your actions can produce the outcomes you desire, you will have little incentive to act or to persevere in the face of difficulties.

Of course, human functioning is influenced by many factors. The success or failure you experience as you engage the countless tasks that comprise your life naturally influences the many decisions you must make. Also, the knowledge and skills you possess will certainly play critical roles in what you choose to do and not do.

"People's level of motivation, emotional states, and actions are based more on what they believe than on what is objectively true. For this reason, how you behave can often be better predicted by the beliefs you hold about your capabilities than by what you are actually capable of accomplishing."

ClaimYourDestiny.global   #ConsciousLeadership

You only need to watch one of the reality TV shows to see how clearly some people are deluded about their own abilities. The opposite is also true — you talk to someone who you know is gifted and they think and believe the complete opposite.

Our upbringing and early influencers, or even a recent happening, have a huge part to play in how and what we believe about ourselves. The great news though is whatever has happened in the past does not have to happen in our future.

These perceptions help determine what you do with the knowledge and skills you have. They also explain why your behaviours are sometimes not matched to your actual capabilities and why your behaviour may differ widely from somebody else, even when you have similar knowledge and skills.

For example, many talented people suffer frequent (and sometimes debilitating) bouts of self-doubt about capabilities they clearly possess, just as many individuals are confident about what they can accomplish despite possessing a modest repertoire of skills. Belief and reality are seldom perfectly matched, and individuals are typically guided by their beliefs when they engage the world.

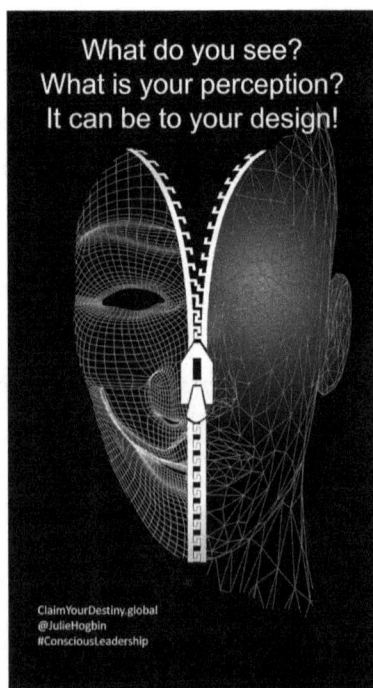

What do you see?
What is your perception?
It can be to your design!

ClaimYourDestiny.global
@JulieHogbin
#ConsciousLeadership

As a consequence, your accomplishments are generally better predicted by your self-perception than by your previous achievements, knowledge, or skills. Of course, no amount of confidence or self-appreciation can produce success when requisite skills and knowledge are absent.

"Skills and knowledge can all be gained if

you want them enough and you find the right mentor to teach you."

ClaimYourDestiny.global   #ConsciousLeadership

COLLECTIVE PERCEPTION

Because individuals operate collectively as well as individually, self-perception is both a personal and a social construct. Collective systems develop a sense of collective effectiveness, it can create the group's shared belief in its capability to attain goals and accomplish desired tasks.

One brain is one but the collective brainpower of a group equals more than the sum of its parts — it's the adage $1+1=3$ or $2+2=5$. However, this is only true when the collective works together in harmony with the same aim. If members of the collective are working against each other one brain doesn't even equate to one — it will function at a lesser capability, as will the individual as they will be experiencing conflict.

For example, organisations develop collective beliefs about the capability of their salesforce to perform, of their managers to teach and otherwise enhance the lives of their workforce, and of their administrators and policymakers to create environments conducive to these tasks. Organisations, as well as individuals, also create beliefs that are not positive — they cannot gain additional sales, clients, revenue, etc. Collectiveness creates a culture which needs to be managed.

Organisations with a strong sense of positive collective perception exercise empowering and vitalising influences over their employees. These effects are evident in their results.

The power of others' attitudes (as mentioned previously) are contagious and will affect your motivation. If you are in the company of a high sender of negative emotion, you will be affected. If you are in the company of a high sender of positivity, it will be less influential.

As the saying goes, it only takes one bad apple to spoil the barrel.

Weed out the bad apples and your motivation will improve. Take on more of the good apples that are doing the same thing that you want to do and your motivation will improve by leaps and bounds.

CHOICES

Only you can justify the choices you make and most of you will make your choices in reference to past experiences rather than future opportunities. Change how you think and you will change your future.

"The definition of insanity is doing the same thing over and over again and expecting a different result."

– Albert Einstein

How do you change to get a different result? It's easy, think differently and take different actions. Open your mind and your being to possibilities; your past does not have to equal your future. With #ConsciousLeadership it can all change.

Every thought, every action, and every decision you make takes you closer to, or further away, from where you want to be. The smallest of decisions compounded over time creates massive change. Rather than attempt to make a huge change overnight, which can be scary and overwhelming, make small incremental changes that lead you towards your goal.

What do I mean? 5 minutes exercise a day wont make much difference if you do or don't do it BUT 5 minutes everyday will. A cake on one day wont make much difference to your health BUT a cake every day will (in the wrong direction). Delaying cutting the lawn for one day wont make much difference BUT delaying every day will.

Even doing nothing takes you further away because everything else is moving forward. The skills of yesteryear will not suffice in the next year. Think about how technology changes. If you haven't kept up with the last change you will soon be a very long way behind!

Sometimes, it can be a life-changing event that allows you to make the decision to do something immediately that you have tried before and failed at. A friend of mine, when diagnosed with cancer, stopped smoking overnight after 40 years. Please do not leave it until that type of thing happens before you change. Take on board #ConsciousLeadership now and change your life for the better, it is your choice!

Start to work now on different decisions for what you want and need:

- Why wait to be taken through a disciplinary process at work before you improve your skills or performance?

- Why wait until you are so over or underweight before you change your nutrition intake?

- Why wait until you cannot walk upstairs without puffing before you increase your fitness level?

- Why wait until you are close to retirement to think about how much money you need to live on and enjoy your retirement?

Through reading, applying, and practicing the experiences of others, you can learn what has worked for those before you, and you can apply those principles in your own life.

Motivational states are directive, they guide behaviours toward satisfying specific goals or specific needs. Do you have clearly defined goals? If you don't, sit down now, identify what it is you really want or need, and write that down. Then create a plan of how you will achieve it. This will provide you with motivation to do things differently.

If you want more information on how to this, I can highly recommend my book 'The Life Changing Magic of Setting Goals'. It is available from Amazon or through ClaimYourDestiny.global

"Change begins with your awareness that your beliefs are a choice; all beliefs, conscious or unconscious, are based on a choice."

ClaimYourDestiny.global   #ConsciousLeadership

There are a myriad of choices to be made all of the time. If you choose a different way to do something, gather information that allows you to make an educated choice for action. Do your research and due diligence and pick the best solution for you.

This will enhance your confidence, create new knowledge, quieten the inner doubting voice, match your values, enhance your beliefs, or question them to bolster your attitude.

This will allow you to convince your unconscious that you are looking after it and it will help you. Provide your unconscious with the reason why you are making alternate choices to that of the past and it will support you all the way.

DELAYED GRATIFICATION

There have been many studies done related to the benefits of delayed gratification. What does this really mean? It means living with the future in mind rather than the present.

In this world of instant gratification, keeping up with the Joneses, wearing the right designer labels, being influenced by adverts that say you must have this face cream and that aftershave, feeling like your holidays must become bigger and more expensive, having to change your car every two years, etc. It can be hard to resist the instant temptation, to be outside the norm, or to exclude yourself from your friends' activities.

In the moment, sometimes it can seem obvious to take the reward, and worry about the future in the future.

Your choice is dependent on your goals, your drivers, your beliefs (and how strong they are), and how strong your will to resist temptation is.

If you can recognise when you have an opportunity for a larger or more important reward, it shows you know the difference between your needs and your wants. When you can recognise these situations, there are key terms you must think of.

Patience, will, and self-control are all characteristics of people who are masters of their environment. One common challenge is postponing immediate gratification in the pursuit of long-term goals. Delayed gratification is the process of transcending immediate temptations to achieve long-term goals.

Knowing how to create, manage, and control your goals is the first step towards completing the things you want most in life; with a goal, we engage our brain to work toward it.

Think of goals as roadmaps designed to keep you on target. They make the experience and the journey possible and more enjoyable. They, in fact, become priorities that drive our actions. They become motivators.

Let me ask you once again:

- What are your long-term goals? And for some of you

- What are your short-term goals?

If you do not have goals sit down now and plan them for yourself, tell yourself and others they are important, write them down and believe you are worthy of them and you will achieve them. Focus on them and they will become a reality

See
Say
Write
Believe
Achieve

ClaimYourDestiny.global

TM

THE POWER OF QUESTIONS

Questions, when constructed in the right way, are the most powerful way to access your beliefs. And this works irrespective of who asks the question. Ask yourself a question and your mind will do its best to provide you with an answer. The better your question, the better the answer.

Do you want to spend the rest of your life figuring out how to get the things you desire, or would you rather put all the guesswork behind you and get down to the fun of building an out-of-this-world lifestyle? Easy choice, right? Then do yourself a favour: suspend your disbelief, lower your shields, and try a simple way of improving your life.

Identify someone you respect who's already experiencing what you're after, find out what questions they habitually ask themselves to achieve those experiences, then use those questions yourself.

This is a globally powerful approach to success that can get you the things you want more quickly than anything else I've discovered. The habitual questions that others ask themselves when asked by yourself, to yourself can transform your life. You don't even need to understand how it all works really, although the answer's quite simple:

"When you change your habitual questions, you change your beliefs, when you change your beliefs, you change your actions, when you change your actions you change your results."

ClaimYourDestiny.global   #ConsciousLeadership

Try it! Take the time to prove to yourself that it works, that it can change the level of pain and pleasure in your life. If you like the results, keep using the questions you've discovered until they become second nature. Do this and you won't care about the why's and the wherefore's. You'll be too busy! You'll have learned firsthand there's nothing more powerful than a good question followed by action.

Ask different questions, and you will end up thinking different thoughts, saying different words, taking different actions, and getting different results. When you go one step further by modeling the questions of successful people, you're helping to ensure that the different results you're pursuing are also good results. In other words, you've done everything you can to arrive at a different place — a good place — to develop different beliefs, which are also profitable beliefs, and to become a different person who is more like the people you admire.

FOCUS

So what does all this mean really?

It means that by looking at why you do what you do and the beliefs behind that, you can basically change the thoughts and motives that direct your behaviour so that you achieve a different result, start a new job, get a promotion, create your own business, leave a relationship, start a relationship, have that difficult conversation, learn to swim, fly a plane, or simply eat a new food; the list is endless.

It is your choice completely — where your focus goes your energy flows — so change your focus to change your results.

Some of our important choices have a timeline. If you delay a decision, the opportunity is gone forever. Sometimes your doubts will stop you from making a choice that involves change and an opportunity may be missed. If you really truly want to change, start now — now is as good a time as any.

Create and ClaimYourDestiny.global through #ConsciousLeadership

My Facebook page and group is ClaimYourDestiny or you can follow me on Twitter @JulieHogbin. Visit ClaimYourDestiny.global for more articles and up to date information, plus various other social media channels and Linkedin. My hashtag is #ConsciousLeadership if you would like to find me.

There are seven days in the week and someday isn't one of them!

ClaimYourDestiny.global
@JulieHogbin
#ConsciousLeadership

Motives and motivation are a matter of choice — yours! Choose well, look at why you believe what you believe, and question it. Listen to the answers of the questions you ask and you will create a different future if you really want to.

My final questions to you are:

- How much do you want to change?

- How willing are you to do what is required?

- What do you need to do right now?

Good luck with whatever it is you want to do. Here's to your fabulous success; you know where to find me.

Julie xx

Immigrating to Success

Self-Leadership Strategies to Manifest Your Life Long Dreams

JACEK SIWEK

I mmigration requires more than interest, it requires commitment. If you want to immigrate to success, commitment is a must.

Some decisions in life make little difference, others will turn your life around entirely. For example, a decision to immigrate is definitely a life-changing decision. I left Poland and immigrated to Canada in 1996. My whole life changed in just one day. I had to learn a new language and culture, gain new friends, learn how to live in a big city, and the list goes on and on. However, there was one more decision I made that had a significant impact on my life. It was the decision to be successful. It wasn't an easy journey, but now that I look back in time, I see how immigrating to another country and changing my life from poverty to success resemble each other remarkably. Allow me to explain.

Immigration is a point of no return. It's not a short visit to see how things will work out. If it gets hard you can't go back. An immigrant makes it happen no matter how hard it gets or how long it takes. It's only when you decide with the same amount of certainty to immigrate to success do you have a chance to transform your life.

Why do people immigrate? Most do it to stop or avoid pain. There's a moment in life when you realize that the past was horrible, the present is even more painful, and the future looks worse. At that moment you decide to change. At that moment there's a psychological shift when you say "No more! Not another day of this! This must change and I must change it!"

If I can teach you any lesson about pain, it would be this: pain is the greatest teacher and motivator of all. If you want to succeed in life, you must first get dissatisfied with your current situation. You must experience massive, immediate, enormous, unbearable amounts of pain in order to be able to come to the moment when you realize "This must change!"

If you aren't where you want to be with your finances CHANGE IT. If you aren't where you want to be with your body weight CHANGE IT. If you aren't happy with your job CHANGE IT. If you aren't happy with your relationship CHANGE IT.

Don't get me wrong, I'm all for making the best out of what we have, but far too often I've seen people who suffer being together. I know it's not easy, but it all comes down to that moment of asking "How long do I want to tolerate it?" In life we get what we tolerate, so if you see something isn't working and you keep tolerating it, nothing will change. You must reach the point of no return, the moment when you decide that not another day will pass by with you living like this. This is the perfect moment when you must immigrate to success. There's no better way.

DEFINE YOUR DESTINATION

In order to reach your goal of immigrating to success you must:

1. Clearly define your goals. Define what you want, not what you don't want. You must know exactly when your goal has been achieved.

2. State what you are committed to do in order to achieve your goals.

3. Name the price you are willing to pay to get there (in terms of time, money, and sacrifice).

4. Get rid of old habits that stop you.

5. Identify what it will cost you not to get to where you want to go. What would be the ultimate pain of not getting there?

6. Define who you want to become as a result of achieving this goal.

If you have all those points done your next step is to educate yourself.

FOUR STAGES OF LEARNING

1. *First, you don't know what you don't know.* For example, you have never seen or heard of a car. How could you learn to drive one? You have no clue what it is. Similarly, you might be ignorant to things that could be useful. Someone else must show you what you don't know. Keep your mind open to other possibilities. Remember, you don't have all the

answers.

2. *Second, you know what you didn't know.* At this stage you're discovering the things you weren't aware of. You don't have any skills yet, but you know what you have to learn in order to succeed. For example, you know what a car is and you've seen people driving one, though you have never driven one yourself. In order for you to learn new skills you must not be afraid to ask for help.

3. *Third, you know what you didn't know and you're actually physically doing it.* At this stage you are actively doing what you know, but it takes your full attention. At this stage it will require your entire focus to complete the task. For example, you know what a car is and you know how to drive it, but it takes your full attention and you aren't capable of doing anything else while driving. Now your focus is on your goal, but it's still outside yourself.

4. *Fourth, you are no longer thinking about what you're doing, you're doing it automatically.* At this stage, because of repetition, your subconscious mind is no longer requiring your full attention and focus. You can do the task while focusing on something else. For example, you can drive, but your focus is on something else. You can have a conversation with somebody sitting next to you. You can listen to the radio or you can plan your next day. Your subconscious mind takes over the complex process of operating a vehicle and simplifies it into one task called driving. We call it second nature because we can perform it without our full attention.

HUMILITY

"Be all that you can be." "You're the best." "You can do anything you put your mind to." "Believe in yourself." "You are worth it." We keep hearing these phrases over and over again. You'll find them on the internet, Facebook, YouTube videos, and inside self-improvement books. But what about humility? What is humility? Humility is not thinking less of yourself, but rather it's thinking of yourself less. Read the above sentence a few times until it sinks in. Humility is the greatest friend in your progress and learning.

In the process of immigrating there's something I refer to as you don't know what you already know. It sounds strange, but I'll give you an example. You are quite capable of asking for directions in your own language. However, when you don't know the foreign language it becomes a challenge. Successful people use different language for the same things. They just sometimes use a sophisticated vocabulary. This kind of thing is common in the financial, medical, and legal industries. So when you start spending time with successful people and they use vocabulary you don't understand, do not be discouraged. Chances are you know exactly what they are talking about, but you simply don't know the verbal representations of the discussed topics. Do not be afraid of asking for clarifications.

I know it is humiliating when learning a new language to ask the same question over and over again. You feel stupid asking for something you think you should know by now. But that fear of appearing stupid, that fear of what people will think if you ask this question again, will prevent you from progressing forward. Recognizing this helped me to learn the language and culture faster than many of my peers at the same time. You must know that you need to put your focus on the other person and ask repeatedly for help until you learn those things necessary to succeed. We have to embarrass ourselves many times and be okay with it. We have to give ourselves time to make mistakes—lots and lots of mistakes. If we do, we will progress 100 times faster than those proud people who are too afraid to sound dumb. That's humility working for you.

Being afraid of making mistakes, and looking stupid because of it, is one of the top reasons people don't succeed. If you study successful people you will see a common pattern. They all make a lot of mistakes, experience plenty of failures, feel a lot of embarrassment, and experience a lot of setbacks. If we want to succeed, we must be ready to accept failure as a major part of our path. However, every time you feel like quitting know that there's another person who already quit right behind you. If you keep going forward, there will be fewer people and less competition simply because the reasons they stopped did not stop you. One of the major reasons why people give up or don't try in the first place is because of fear of being humiliated. They don't want people to criticize them, and they don't want people to make fun of them. Nobody does. But the truth is this is your life, and there will always be people who will make fun of you. There will always be people who'll think badly of you, criticize you, and point the finger at you. It's absolutely inevitable. Remember, humility is all about thinking of yourself less, rather than thinking less of yourself.

DIRT REMOVAL

"Bad habits are easier to abandon today than tomorrow."
– Proverb

This step is a must, but you may not appreciate its value until you start putting it in practice. Every house that ever got built started with someone's vision, then a blueprint was made. As much as most want to see the completed version of their beautiful kitchen or bathroom, the first step of construction is removal of dirt. In order to build solid foundations, you must remove all loose soil. You want to build up but first you must go down to the solid place that will not move when storms and winters come. Removal of dirt in your life is no different. We all have it and we must get rid of as much of it as we can in order to build ourselves based on solid value.

Here are some things that might be in your life that aren't allowing you to build the life you want to have:

1. Negative people and their negative comments and criticisms

2. Media. Example: Constant Negative News (CNN)

3. Time wasters: games, social media, TV, excessive entertainment

4. Unfinished projects (like a book you started reading and haven't finished)

5. Disorganized messes (like keys you've never used and don't even know what they're for)

6. Junk food

Removing dirt from your life comes down to one word: STANDARD. You have a standard in life that you'll not go below. A standard is nothing more than a line in the sand that says "I'm not willing to go below this. It's unacceptable, and I refuse to tolerate it." In life we will get what we tolerate, so setting up a minimum standard is a necessity. When I immigrated, all I had with me was one suitcase with summer clothes. When you immigrate, you have to be careful about what you take with you because your allowance for your luggage is limited. At the same time, you'll realize just how few things you really need and that leaving stuff behind might be one of the best things that could happen to free you from having to deal with unnecessary time wasters.

In your new country of success there's simply no space for time wasting activities and negative people.

COMMUNICATE TO INFLUENCE

Every person who ever immigrated to another country knows how difficult it is until they learn the language people use to communicate. If you can't speak the language, your communication will be extremely limited, and as a result your life will always be a struggle. In fact, should someone ask me what the number one skill in life is, I will say without hesitation: "You must master communication skills in order to be successful."

Think about it for a moment. Show me one aspect of your life where proper communication isn't required in order to be successful. If you want to be a successful parent, you must first learn how to communicate with your children. If you want to be a successful spouse, you must learn how to communicate with your partner. If you want to be successful in business, you must learn how to effectively communicate with your customers, employees, business partners, investors, and the list goes on.

However, the most important person you must master communication with is yourself. You have to learn how to communicate with yourself in order to stay motivated, focused, driven, dedicated, and committed. You must know what works for you and what doesn't. You must become a student of yourself first before you learn what motivates others. Language is what connects people, but lack of it separates them. You should put in the effort necessary to learn what you need to know in order to become an effective communicator. Who is an effective communicator? It's a person who can influence others to take action. In order to influence you need to learn how to connect with others first, which means you have to learn how to develop rapport.

MAGIC OF RAPPORT

The key to rapport lies in one word: commonality. I can summarize this skill with one sentence: people like each other when they're like each other. The more you have in common with others the easier it is to develop rapport. Maybe you had a situation when you met someone for the first time and you kept asking questions to find something in common. If you found nothing, then the conversation became awkward and most likely died. Maybe you've known someone for many years and still can't find anything in common, so each time you see each other you feel like you are total strangers. However, I'm also sure you've had a moment in life when you met someone for the first time and instantly felt a connection. After a short period of time you felt like you had known that person forever. Why does that happen? Well, you simply saw yourself in the other person. You liked them because they were like you or they were similar to someone you already liked.

This is all based on commonality. Your subconscious mind will quickly pick up on all the similarities between the person you just met and yourself. If you know nothing of the person you just met, all you have to do is match and mirror them as closely as you can. Immediately match their physiology by copying their body language. If they sit on a chair, you sit on a chair. If they lean forward, you lean forward. If they have crossed legs, you cross yours. Simply match and mirror what they do and their mind will soon start picking up a signal that you are just like them. As soon as they start speaking, match their speaking pattern. If they speak slow, you speak slow. If they speak fast, you speak with the same tempo. You might be afraid they'll notice what you are doing and will accuse you of mimicking them. Truthfully, they won't notice. Especially because they don't know you yet and they don't know your natural behavior. Therefore, the more you copy them the quicker rapport will be developed.

If you use this method daily, sooner or later it will become second nature and you'll be able to develop rapport with people instantaneously without ever worrying about what you'll have to say or how to behave.

PAIN OF LETTING GO

"Sometimes we have to let go of what is good in order to be great."
– Unknown

This moment hits every immigrant on the planet: feeling homesick. It can be missing loved ones, friends, familiar places, or favorite TV shows in your own language. I was not immune to it. I fell in love with a girl right before I immigrated and I missed her a lot. I missed my best friend and our daily walks to school. I missed my town and the street I grew up on. Most of all I missed the feeling of belonging. Everyone has to go through it, but it doesn't make it easier just because others feel the same pain. There were many moments when I felt like just jumping on a plane and going back. Feeling like you want to quit because you feel like you don't belong is normal and eventually will fade away. When you realize that you no longer want to live a life of poverty you'll have to let go of many things, including the ones you love. During the really tough moments when I worked 14 hour days delivering flyers for $2.50 per hour (minimum wage was $8) I kept in mind one thought that kept me going. In order to be great you have to let go of what is good. There's a price to pay for everything and when you immigrate to a new country or to success you will pay a price. There'll be people in your life who were your close friends, and now that you're having success, they won't want to be around you or you won't want to be around them. There'll be people who'll not be happy about your success, not because they don't care about you but because they don't want to be left behind. You'll discover that people who claimed to be your close friends are now starting to see you as an opportunity for their own gain. There'll be moments when you might want to sabotage your success because you'll feel that it's not worth the trouble you're having. But, if you give up struggling for your success, you'll never get there and as a result, you'll never help anyone else to get there either.

Success comes with a price tag and in order to get it there's no other way than to pay the price. However, there's a moment when you'll know how great of a decision you've made by leaving your old way of living and deciding to immigrate. It's the moment when you go back for a visit. After five years of being in Canada, I finally got my papers, so I decided to go back to Poland for a visit. I was sure that all my peers would be far ahead of me because the previous five years I had spent learning how to live again from scratch. Surely a new language, culture, school, group of friends, etc. would have caused me to grow slower than my peers who kept on going. Or so I thought. When I went back, I quickly realized how much I had grown. I saw how many people were still stuck in the same place and had done nothing with their life. If anything, many were worse off than they had been five years previously. This short visit gave me a lot to think about. All of a sudden all the things I missed had smaller value. I still missed my friends and family, but I knew that if I stayed with them my life would never grow forward at the speed it was growing.

One day we went climbing mountains in Poland and came up with an idea to go see Mount Everest the following weekend. Surely enough, the next weekend we were in Nepal looking at the tallest mountain, riding elephants in a jungle, and trekking in one of the most beautiful regions in the world. My peers couldn't even dream about such an adventure. It was then that I realized it all comes down to answering one question: Is it worth it? If the answer is yes, then simply make a decision, find out what it takes, and go for it.

You've most likely heard of people saying that true friends are found in need. Pain or trouble in life will show who your true friends are. There is truth to that, however, success will show you the same. If someone is your true friend, they'll be happy for you when they see you succeeding. Those are the friends you should keep and cherish. Focus on what you've gained and what the true rewards are for your hard work. Your pain of regret will disappear.

ADAPTING TO A NEW CULTURE

"Well, the thing that I learned as a diplomat is that
human relations ultimately make a huge difference."
– Madeleine Albright, the first female U.S. Secretary of State

When you listen to many motivational speakers, some of the most common advice they'll give you is: You have to stand out. You have to be different. You can't be average. Break some rules, etc. There is definitely truth to that, but what they rarely tell you is that in order for you to become valuable you must first learn, practice, and master the fundamentals. What that means is when you immigrate to a new culture you have to learn how they live and do things before you introduce anything new. Simply put, you have to fit in before you stand out.

Gold fish will grow proportionally to the size of the container you put them in. The bigger the container the bigger the fish will grow. We, too, adapt. We want to fit in and be accepted by those we love. Fitting in is by far one of the most powerful internal motivators we have. I'm sure you've heard that we become the average of five of our closest friends. This is a very true statement. Adapting to a new culture first requires choosing the right culture for you. Your friends will create pressure inside you. This internal pressure will become a driving force for you and it could serve you or destroy you.

When a young person goes through army training, they'll often adopt standards and discipline like nowhere else. Very often they'll even keep making their bed and polishing their shoes when they go home where there's no one to ask them to do these things. However, the more time passes the more such useful habits fade away. Why does this happen? Many studies show that people become what their peer group expects them to. That's why choosing the right peer group is so important. This piece of information is so crucial that if you forgot everything else in this chapter and only learned and applied this one principle, your chances of success would be much greater than if you applied everything else in this chapter except this rule.

Nobody successful builds anything meaningful by themselves. You must learn how to build a team of people who have the same vision and surround yourself with those who'll support you on your goals. There's simply no other way. The question is: How do you find people who live in a "successful country?"

Here are some of the things that successful people do versus those who are not:

SUCCESSFUL PEOPLE	UNSUCCESSFUL PEOPLE
Read every day	Watch TV every day
Compliment	Criticize
Embrace change	Fear change

SUCCESSFUL PEOPLE	UNSUCCESSFUL PEOPLE
Forgive others	Hold a grudge
Talk about ideas	Talk about people
Continuously learn	Think they know it all
Accept responsibility for their failures	Blame others for their failures
Have a sense of gratitude	Have a sense of entitlement
Set goals and develop a written life plan	Never set goals
Journal	Claim they journal but never do
Set a budget	Never set a budget
Save money	Spend money rashly
Have mentors and coaches	Have friends to entertain themselves
Hope others will succeed	Hope others will fail
Operate from a transformational perspective	Operate from a transactional perspective
Give other people credit for their victories	Take all the credit for their victories
Share information and data	Hold information and data
Know who they are and who they are not	Not sure who they are
Know their purpose	Don't know their purpose
Exude joy	Exude anger
Wake up early, go to bed early	Wake up late, go to bed late
Listen to educational programs	Listen to news
In control of their life	Out of control of their life
Manage energy	Manage time
Make to be lists	Make to do lists
Certain, focused, outcome oriented	Uncertain, confused, excuses oriented
On track	Lost

SUCCESSFUL PEOPLE	UNSUCCESSFUL PEOPLE
Know realistically where they are in life and where they want to be at a specific point in time	They think they are much further in life than reality and don't know where they want to be
Take care of their body	Pay attention to their body when they get sick
Anticipate change	React to change
They lead by example	They demand from others
They appreciate others, expect from themselves	They expect of others, appreciate nobody
Build themselves by building others	Try to build themselves by putting others down
Train, practice, memorize	Hope to improvise
They say: Thank you for…(doing or being something specific)	They say: Thank you for everything
Know what they want and focus on it	Know what they don't want and focus on it
Speak the truth with consequence	Justify, talk about excuses, lie to get away
Pay full attention	Distracted
They see challenges in life that make them stronger	They see problems in life that make them weaker
Over deliver and exceed people's expectations	Overpromise and under deliver
They keep changing to get better results	They stay the same expecting better results
If something must change I have to change it	If something must change someone else must change it for me
They celebrate their successes	They celebrate holidays only
They have a story of becoming a victor	They have a story of becoming a victim

As you can see these are two different cultures with different beliefs, values, rituals, and habits. The items in the "successful list" are the fundamentals that must be learned and practiced in your network. You might not be able to check off all the things on the list, but the more you do and the more you put them into practice, the quicker you will get where you want to go.

SHORTCUTS THAT SLOW THINGS DOWN

"Strength and growth come only through continuous effort and struggle."
– Napoleon Hill

What do you think will help you learn a new language: a dictionary or an electronic translator? Many choose the electronic translator because of speed and convenience. Unfortunately, it slows down their progress and impedes their ability to memorize necessary words. Personally, I noticed I had to check a new word two to three times in a dictionary in order to remember it. The electronic translator did the thinking for me so I had to translate the same word many times and even after translating it eight or ten times it still wouldn't stick in my memory. Today, we can use GPS, Google, smart phones, etc., and they're truly great tools. However, they don't train us. By using them our skills aren't getting stronger, they're getting weaker. It's like going to the gym and asking someone to lift the weights for you in the hope that you will develop muscles.

In business, to become an expert, you must start by becoming an apprentice. There's no shortcut. Although, if you just read the headlines on social media, I'm sure you'll find countless examples of people promising you how to become rich instantly by following some simple, secret formula. The truth is, success requires hard work. You must also determine what kind of work is worth your effort. Far too many people fall into the trap of thinking that hard work will bring them success. All you have to do is go to a third world country and watch people working on farms to know this isn't true. They aren't rich but they work very hard.

In business, you will find story after story of people trying to scam others by overcharging and not delivering the value they promised. I have never met a person who successfully scammed others long-term. It's all about producing value in other people's lives. It's about delivering more than what people expect. It's about making someone's life better by creating value for those who need it. There's no shortcut. That's why so many businesses go bankrupt in a very short time. They don't want to take the time to build a brand with a solid foundation that represents value. When the storm hits, they get wiped out.

The struggle is real and in order to succeed you have to invest in yourself. It's by far the most important investment you will ever make. Create a map of what it takes to be successful. Go to school, take courses, read books, go to seminars, take on an apprenticeship, and acquire certifications. I don't know what it will take for you to become successful, but whatever it is you must make a point of identifying where you are, where you want to be, and the best path to get there. You don't have to learn everything, but you do need to know the things you can't outsource to others.

Creating a team is very important and hiring people will definitely be part of your success, but don't expect to just hire people to do things for you and hope they will create success for you. If you want success you have to become a leader, and leaders walk first.

There is one investment that will save you time, money, and lots of frustrations. It's the only "shortcut" that I know of that actually works. It's called modelling.

MODELLING SUCCESS IS THE NEW TIME MACHINE

"Remembering that I'll be dead soon is the most important tool I've ever encountered to help me make the big choices in life. Because almost everything—all external expectations, all pride, all fear of embarrassment or failure—these things just fall away in the face of death, leaving only what is truly important."
– Steve Jobs

Wisdom comes from experience. Experience comes from making mistakes and learning from them. The more mistakes you make, the wiser you will become. But, it's always better to learn from other people's mistakes. Coaching or mentoring can save you decades of mistakes. If you don't have money or connections to successful people, then books and biographies of those who inspire you is a great place to start.

There's access to almost anything we want at our fingertips and we can use NET (No Extra Time) to acquire this knowledge. Listen to audio books in the car, for example. Just add to your existing routine. Don't waste time by learning through trial and error, that's how our parents learned. We simply don't have that much time to waste. Time is our greatest commodity and it should never be wasted. You think you have time but the greatest lesson from death is that you don't. There's no reset button. There's no way of going back and there's no reason to waste your life on unnecessary activities. How much is your time worth? If you're wasting lots of time on a job you hate and at home you only watch TV to escape reality, then you are committing a slow suicide. That's right, your time is limited.

IF YOU KILL YOUR TIME, YOU'RE KILLING YOUR LIFE!

Don't try to be smarter than experts. Follow everything they do until you become an expert yourself, then you can start breaking some rules. Imagine, someone spent 20 years writing a book by gathering the best possible information from their life experience and then you read it in just a few days or sometimes hours. You can compress decades into days by learning from the masters. Can you imagine someone learning computer programming without any guidance? By the time they master the program, their skills will no longer be useful because a new program will take its place. We live in times when we no longer have the luxury of learning slowly. Businesses go bankrupt and get downsized and outsourced every day. Mostly, it's because they failed to innovate and hire consultants that could get them to the new goal faster. Someone else did and beat them to it. Today, making the best use of your time is what makes the difference between winning or losing, between succeeding and failing, between thriving and getting by.

The point of all this talk about time is simple: If you cherish your life and want to be successful, you must have a mentor or a coach. A mentor will give you a totally new perspective on things and could save you years of your life and lots of money in the process. No matter how smart you think you are, you're limited by your opinion and your own perspective. If you watch professional athletes, they all, without exception, have coaches. All famous actors, musicians, politicians, business owners, etc. have coaches and mentors. Many of them have multiple coaches at the same time simply because they know the value of it. Why reinvent the wheel if you can learn from someone who already made all the mistakes and walked the path you want to walk?

If you're serious about success, then you must immigrate to it. If you value your life, get a mentor.

Should you wish to learn more, contact Jacek Siwek at **immigratetosuccess@gmail.com** or visit his website at **www.immigratetosuccess.com**

Bringing Balance
to Your Life

DENNIS GARRIDO

When I woke up in the hospital staring up into the terrified eyes of someone I cared about, after my second cardiac arrest in one year, I knew that things had to change in my life. Especially because I was only in my twenties at the time.

Everything in my life was out of balance. Obviously, physically because I was lying in the emergency room, but more importantly my mind, emotions, and spirit were completely out of whack, and that had taken a toll on my body.

Now you may be wondering how someone so young could have had two cardiac arrests before the age of 30? It won't be hard to imagine once I share my story with you. I wish I could tell you that I had a great upbringing, one filled with laughter and love, but it wasn't.

At age eleven I was removed from my parent's home by The Children's Aid Society because they deemed my parents unfit to raise me. During that time, I went through a whirlwind of emotions. A part of me was happy that change was finally occurring, because clearly at that point, the way things were, wasn't working at all.

Another part of me felt fear because of the unknown. I didn't know exactly where I would be living, nor did I know for sure what my group & foster homes would be like, what the other kids would be like, what the living conditions would be like, how far or close I'd be to my family and hometown, etc. Essentially, I wasn't 100% certain nor 100% convinced that I was going into better circumstances.

Also, I felt sad, since I wouldn't see my parents or siblings anymore, nor my home town and many of the people whom I'd see on a regular basis; everything FAMILIAR would be gone! Lastly, I felt angry, that it had come to me being removed from my parent's house, away from those who were in my life for all those years. As twisted and messed up as it may be, I was angry that I was leaving a life that I had become accustomed to and felt somewhat comfortable in (comfortable in comparison to the unknown that lay ahead); and most of all, angry that I was leaving FAMILIARITY!!!!

Please understand me, I am no longer angry at my parents, and you shouldn't be either. They did the best they could, but when you are broken yourself, unless you find a way out, you will repeat what had been bestowed on you from the previous generations. I can be thankful because what I went through helped create the person I am today and as a coach, it gives me great empathy and understanding to be able to help others. So, don't feel sorry for me because even though my life had a rough start, I get to choose the rest of it and it is going to be GREAT!!!

THE NEXT SEVEN YEARS OF MY LIFE

For the next seven years until I turned 18, I was bounced from foster/group home to foster/group home. I rarely spent more than three months at any one place, and it caused some major emotional setbacks that took me a long time to overcome.

One of the biggest negative emotional setbacks was again to do with familiarity. As I spent time with those at my new home, seeing them every day and coming to know them personally; I naturally formed a connection/friendship with them. It seemed that no sooner had I done that; they were removed from my life. People whom I really liked (a few of them, whom I loved), ALL GONE!!! Which basically solidified my already ingrained defence mechanism of keeping distant from others; not allowing anyone to get close enough to form any connection with me.

Inevitably, this made it very difficult for me to form any type of relationship with anyone. School and extracurricular activities were hard because I never knew how long I would be staying in one place. What was the point of making friends if I could never keep them? It was a lot easier to keep my distance than to reach out yet again and have everything torn away from me.

Eventually, I started to tear down the wall that prevented me from getting too close to anyone. To this day, the negative emotional setbacks I experienced, still affect me to some degree; though I CHOOSE not to allow them to prevent me from forming meaningful relationships!

THE DARKEST TIME OF MY LIFE

All that change led to one of the darkest periods of my life. Emotionally and mentally I had shut down and could no longer function. Life was so hard. Even things that were simple, now became agonizingly difficult and it hit the point where I didn't want to live anymore. What was the use of carrying on in this horrible life when there wasn't any hope of it changing?

My life began to narrow down to one permanent solution, and that was to end it all by committing suicide. I just couldn't handle life anymore, but I truly believe that Almighty God, the universe or whatever you want to call it, had a bigger plan for me. Even though I tried several times, I just couldn't die!!! Because of those attempts, I ended up in psychiatric institutions, a few times.

It finally came to the point where I was tired of trying to die, I was tired of institutions and I was weary from all the self-harm, and so I came to a decision. I guess you could say that it was a turning point in my life; I wasn't going to attempt suicide anymore. I wasn't sure what to do because my circumstances hadn't changed, but I was willing to look for options. That was the beginning point of change in my life. The will to live!!!

IT DIDN'T GET BETTER RIGHT AWAY

Life is a journey with twists, hills, and valleys of varying shapes and sizes, with occasional points where you make decisions that put you on a different path. The determination not to kill myself had set me on a new road, but I still didn't know what to do or which way to go. It was slow going as I fumbled my way through, but at least I was moving forward!!!

At age 18 I was no longer in the custody of The Children's Aid Society, so, I moved back with my parents, which was the perfect testing grounds for me to apply the life lessons I had learned so far. You would be amazed by how much maturity one can have at 18 when you have been through what I have. It wasn't easy, and it was hard work, but I managed to re-establish a relationship with my parents and not only complete high school, but also graduate from post-secondary schooling.

One of the things I had decided to do was get my student loans paid off in the six-month grace period, which I managed to do; but in doing so, I pushed myself way beyond my physical limits which brought on the first cardiac arrest.

You would think I would have learned from that first experience, but I didn't, and less than a year later we are back to the beginning of this chapter waking up in the hospital from my second one.

This time I learned my lesson and chose a different path, but I still didn't know how to achieve what I needed. For so long I had lived in imbalance, that I didn't know where to start, but the catalyst for change was just around the corner.

I FINALLY REALIZED WHAT BALANCE WAS

Believe it or not, it is the simplest things that can bring about the most profound changes in life. My search for balance in my life had begun, and it is amazing how the answer came; by a knock at my door one day.

That day I was busy working on something, so when the first knock came, I ignored it. It was only after a couple of rings of the doorbell that I finally decided that I would answer it. There was a well-dressed gentleman at the door and even though I don't remember most of what he said, one thing became clear, I was missing an essential element to finding the balance I craved. Now, I knew what it was. You can only find balance when you address ALL the areas of your life, and I had been missing one. The spiritual side.

It is amazing what happens when you finally have all the pieces together. As I started to study the Bible, I finally could build a solid spiritual foundation, that enabled me to re-evaluate things in my life, and thus, put a plan together to create balance in my life. In the rest of this chapter, I am going to share with you what I learned.

Just before I do that, I do want to mention one thing. All of this is a process. Can I say that I am 100% balanced in my life? No, but when I started at 3-4% and then jumped to 85%, I think that is very good growth. It's difficult to attain 100% balance in every aspect of one's life, that is why even the most successful people keep learning and growing. So, the goal is not perfection, but growth. As long as you are continuing to move forward, that is all that matters.

7 STEPS TO BRING BALANCE TO YOUR LIFE

Here's one of the things that I have learned about bringing balance to your life. In some ways, it is easy. The steps I am going to teach you are simple to understand. The hard part is training yourself to be aware of it every day and live by it. The good thing is, though it may be hard at first, the more you practice it, the easier it gets.

STEP 1

Ask yourself, "What are my priorities in life?" You want to look at it from all aspects of your life, personal and professional. In terms of personal that includes goals physically, emotionally, mentally, spiritually, relationships (such as your spouse or significant other), family and friends. You want to look at it from the point of what you need and what you want. For each one, you should have one to two priorities.

In terms of professional, they can include your current work situation and areas of improvement there, plus plan for your future. Put down both needs and wants.

	NEEDS	WANTS
P E R S O N A L		
P R O F E S S I O N A L		

STEP 2

Look at your needs column. What are the most important priorities personally and professionally? It is important that you only start out working on a few at a time. If you try to do everything at once, you will become overwhelmed and quit. Then, figure out the things you need to do to get those needs met.

STEP 3

Now go through your wants and do the same thing as Step 2 above. Don't overlook this. Part of having balance in life is having both your needs and wants met. Obviously, your needs are more important, but without the wants, you give up hope.

STEP 4

Set up a timeline for those needs to be accomplished. What are you going to do today, this week, this month, this year, and in the next five years to bring yourself to reach those priorities?

STEP 5

Do the same thing for your wants. Set up your timeline of completion.

STEP 6

DO THE ACTIONS. Here is where the rubber meets the road. You can plan and plan and plan, but if there is no action involved you will be in the same place, with the same problems, five years from now.

STEP 7

Re-evaluate. Every few months go back through this whole process again.

As you grow and change, so will your priorities, your needs and your wants.

THE BEST WAY TO ACCOMPLISH THIS

Very rarely can a person accomplish this alone. Have you ever heard the saying, "You can't see the forest for the trees?" That is what happens in our lives. We get so caught up in the unimportant things right in front of us, that we miss the big picture and we don't recognize growth when it occurs.

Now, you do have several options. One is to have family members try to help you through this. While you do need their support, they are usually looking at the same trees you are and can miss things.

Two, you can go to friends for help. They do tend to see more of the big picture, but many times they can't give you the encouragement and motivation you need at times to get past yourself.

Three, you work with a professional who knows how to help you bring balance to your life. They can come alongside of you and guide you to the quickest path to success because there will be obstacles that try to stop you. Did I forget to mention that?

No road to balance is smooth; little pebbles will get into your shoes to irritate you and take your focus off your goals. Barriers will be put up that you will have to learn how to go over, under, around or through. People will get in your way and tell you that it is the wrong road to take and you should follow them. All sorts of things will try to keep you from what you want.

Coaches are keen observers who can not only help you with what is going on right now, but they have been down your road and they know what is up ahead and can keep you moving forward, even when everything is telling you to stop.

That is what I'm offering to be for you. Let me help you on your path to balance in your life. I have been on both sides of the coin, and I can guide you through the roughest parts. I can relate to what you are feeling and am more than willing to help you navigate this wonderful thing called life.

First of all, if you would like more information on how to start this process, you can pre-order my upcoming book at www.dennisgarrido.com Second, you can email me at dennis@dennisgarrido.com and request your free 15-minute phone consultation where we can discuss your situation and see if we are a good fit for each other. Third, maybe you realize more people need to hear this message. I am also available to speak to groups and conferences. If so, just send me an email, and we can arrange a time to speak.

No matter what you decide, know this. You can achieve balance in your life. It is possible. I can tell you that it has been worth everything I went through to get to this point. The peace I experience now, compared to the chaos I lived before, is so amazing and I wish the same for you.

Don't miss out. Make the choice to change your life today, and I guarantee that you won't regret it!!!

Are You Sick of Bad Behavior? Awaken the Hero Within!

LINDA K. WONG

"Common sense, common courtesy and common decency really do have a lot in common. They all disappeared around the same time."

— Susan Gale

SOCIAL NORMS AND COMMON DECENCY

Is there something in the water?

I feel compelled to write about the state of human behavior, as I am not sure when it all went wrong. It seems like I woke up one day, looked around, and the world had suddenly gone crazy.

As a child, my parents taught me manners and respect. I learned to be considerate, polite, and kind to others. I read social cues and was aware of the apparent social norms because those things related to behavior that was expected from me, just as other behaviors were not tolerated. Elders and community leaders were good role models who taught me how to get along in the world and instilled in me a sense of pride and decency.

Somewhere along the way though, these social norms have disintegrated. Perhaps it was with the advent of social media. Perhaps it was from watching reality TV stars misbehave. Perhaps it was when parenting norms changed, as parents stopped teaching their children accountability. Perhaps it was due to the increasing tribalism that we see within our divisive politics. Or, perhaps it began a while ago, but it was so subtle that we did not notice the changes right away.

Our ability to communicate, and move goods (or people), tremendously improved our lives as we entered the Digital Age. We began to see monumental innovations in technology and infrastructure. Therefore, I can't help but wonder if we are taking people for granted. Has it become too easy to communicate with our friends who are living abroad?

The irony is that with increased communication capabilities, we have lost an aspect of our humanity. How often do you see couples having dinner in a restaurant, ignoring each other as they communicate with others on their smartphones? Or a group of teenagers, glued to their mobile devices instead of being present and enjoying the company of their friends? How about you? When was the last time you had lunch with a friend and found yourself becoming a slave to your text messages or Facebook account?

All of this behavior would have been considered rude and unacceptable not that long ago. But, like pebbles skipping across a pond, each of these shifts in behaviors and attitudes created a ripple in our homes, our workplaces, our schools, our communities, and more importantly, our relationships. Every time we learn to tolerate and accept lousy behavior, the limits continue to be stretched.

I don't know about you, but I am tired of feeling like I have no control over this world that continues to become unhinged. I am surrounded by people behaving badly, and "I'm done."

I'm done having to stand idly by as our children become products of a harsh and unloving environment. I'm done with becoming engulfed in a world that seems to be losing its moral compass. I'm done waking up with an overwhelming sense of dread, anticipating to witness, or hear about, more examples of indecency or cruelty. I'm done noticing people become cold, unloving, and uncaring to their friends and neighbors. I'm done feeling powerless, watching bad behavior escalate, and being unable to do anything about it.

What are you done with? What bad behavior gets underneath your skin? Before we can make a change, it is essential to recognize what behaviors we are okay with, and which are no longer acceptable. After all, you can't change what you do not acknowledge.

Later in this chapter, I will get into the positive changes and movements that are taking place around the globe, the stages of change, and more importantly, what YOU can do to awaken the hero within yourself. I have also included a fun five-question quiz on how to know if you are friends with someone who is wretched (feel free to substitute your own adjective!). But, first, I want to address how bad things have become.

Now, before you dive deep into the current state of affairs, I want you to know that if at any time it feels too much, too negative, or too overwhelming, then please skip forward to the parts where I tell you how it can get better! How, together, we can create a positive future for us all!

"You are the captain of your *own* ship; don't let anyone else take the wheel."

— Michael Josephson

THE STATE OF UGLINESS AND HATE

Our tolerance and acceptance of anger, vitriol, and hate is growing worse with each passing day. But, where is the motivation to do better – or be better?

Even our role models are behaving poorly! Famous actors, sports figures, politicians, and even spiritual leaders are no longer illustrating positive examples for their communities, or society as a whole. They seem to render little restraint when tweeting negative, or mean-spirited, messages, even though thousands, or even millions, of people will read it.

Catherine Steiner-Adair, a psychologist and author, said that this behavior from our leaders is already hurting our children. "When we tolerate leaders — in the popular media like a Kardashian, or a president — behaving in this way, we are creating a very dangerous petri dish for massive cultural change."[1]

Moreover, it is difficult to avoid the polarizing and divisive state of politics, no matter what country you live in. Nationalism is becoming popular, and since Donald Trump won the United States presidency in 2016, there has been a rise in hate crimes in the U.S. According to the Washington Post, "American politics seem to have raised the rhetorical flourishes to a new level

---

1 https://apnews.com/2e5fcbca8c084450bbb7971f235f9b2e

and also brought a troubling question to the surface: At what point does all the alarmist talk of civil war actually increase the prospect of violence, riots or domestic terrorism?"[2]

WHY WE DO THE THINGS WE DO

We have become so vain and self-centered! According to Psychology Today, "Societal trends have drifted away from an emphasis on community and the common good and moved toward the need to take care of self, perfect oneself, even to the point of self-aggrandizement."[3]

In addition to being vain and self-centered, we have become apathetic, as we often stand by and do nothing to stop bad behavior in its tracks. Is the Bystander Effect at play here? The Bystander Effect refers to a phenomenon where individuals in a group of people do not help someone in distress. It's been shown that people are more likely to take action when there are few people, or no one else, available to help out. There are two reasons for this. The first is that being in a group diffuses the sense of responsibility; people feel like someone else will jump in to help since the responsibility to act is shared among everyone in the group. The second reason is that when other observers fail to act, it sends an unconscious signal to the rest that they do not need to act either.

SoulPancake, an innovative project that tackles the universality of the human experience, posts their often shocking and emotional social experiments

---

2 https://www.washingtonpost.com/politics/in-america-talk-turns-to-something-unspoken-for-150-years-civil-war/2019/02/28/b3733af8-3ac4-11e9-a2cd-307b06d0257b_story.html?noredirect=on&utm_term=.1db6a4ec54eb
3 https://www.psychologytoday.com/ca/blog/when-the-media-is-the-parent/201401/self-centered-the-new-normal

on their YouTube channel[4]. In 2011, *SoulPancake* conducted an ingenious experiment demonstrating how the Bystander Effect, the science of empathy, impacted a group of young people who thought they were there to give their opinions on products. But, the real test was to see if they would help the facilitator who was struggling to set up his product demonstration. As anticipated by the team, who secretly filmed the experiment, when there was a large group, it took a long time for someone to help out, but as the group became smaller, someone volunteered more quickly to help.

There are a myriad of reasons for bad, rude, or disrespectful behavior. But, I believe that people misbehave because they can. Their behavior works for them in some way, and those around them tolerate it, or the behavior would have stopped. I believe these 'bad operators' need to feel superior or have power over others. They do it because it makes them feel good. They may even receive recognition and validation from their peers for their bad behavior, which encourages them to continue acting badly. This is, unfortunately, becoming all too common in the online community, which I will discuss next.

Then there are the people who infrequently engage in negative behavior. In a recent study, "Anticipating and Resisting the Temptation to Behave Unethically," by the University of Chicago, researchers found that "people are more likely to engage in unethical behavior if they believe the act is an isolated incident and if they don't think about it ahead of time."

If you are feeling a bit riled up after reading about so much bad behavior, then rest assured, you are normal. The worst thing for us is to become desensitized to the ugliness taking place in our society. Worry not, as I have faith that goodness will prevail!

---

4 https://www.youtube.com/user/soulpancake

OUR ONLINE BEHAVIOR AFFECTS OUR EVERYDAY LIVES

Whoever coined the term "sticks and stones may break my bones, but names will never hurt me," did not anticipate how gut-wrenchingly painful it can be to suffer through aggressive words coming at you like daggers. Communication can be used cruelly, and words can cause pain and inflict harm on their intended recipient.

Because we live in a digital age, where what we see online permeates into our everyday lives, it's challenging to separate bad behavior that exists on social media, from that which exists face-to-face.

"Over time, the attitudes and behaviors that we are concerned with right now in social media will bleed out into the physical world," said Dr. Karen North, a psychologist and director of the University of Southern California's Digital Social Media Program. It's true!

Mainstream media now reports on the tweets of famous people and politicians. It has somehow become newsworthy. Cruel and humiliating posts often become "an instant hit online," going viral, being played by mainstream and social media, making it difficult to ignore, says psychologist Dr. Catherine Steiner-Adair. She goes on to say that when we don't make it clear that we do not condone the cruel or disgusting behavior, "we are creating a bystander culture where people think this is funny."

Cruelty is not funny! Body shaming and other types of shaming occur online every day. It is out of control. Hiding behind the anonymity of social media, individuals partake in name-calling with derogatory terms such as "fat" and "ugly." This abhorrent behavior is unacceptable. Since when is shaming people publicly, or at all for that matter, acceptable? After all, beauty is in the eye of the beholder; we are not here to judge others – we are here to love. If my fellow humans think this behavior is okay, then we have, as a society, become unhinged.

Consequently, mean people are becoming popular. Can you imagine? I presume unless and until we all turn off our TVs, or stop the streaming media on our digital devices, mainstream media will continue to report on famous people behaving badly. When we tune out, we send a message to media and news conglomerates that we no longer wish to support and encourage this behavior.

After all, social conventions are arbitrary rules and norms that govern our daily behavior. It has become an unconscious mode of engaging with others. Sure, we follow laws to avoid going to jail. But we also do what is expected of us, such as saying good morning to our colleagues, holding the door open for the person behind us, or giving our seat to a pregnant woman or elderly person on public transportation. These norms we learned growing up, and just assumed that they would be passed onto the next generation to carry on. However, we have become a global tribe of mean people! Unless and until we do something to cease the lunacy, and restore normalcy, it will continue. And not just continue, but the meanness will propagate into our workplaces, where some level of normality remains.

If you saw a tourist prancing on top of flowers or destroying nature for a selfie, what would you do? One weekend in March 2019, nearly 150,000 tourists overran a California town to get a glimpse of a super bloom, a rare occurrence of orange poppies blanketing the hillsides. Officials were forced to close the canyon due to the chaos, which became a public safety crisis. Many of these tourists walked through the poppies to get their Instagram pic, with total disregard for the flowers.[5] This is an example of how vanity and self-

5 https://globalnews.ca/news/5071689/california-super-bloom-selfie/

centeredness get in the way of common sense. Would you walk on top of a beautiful flowerbed in front of your mother? Since when did this behavior become okay?

Have you heard the expression "two wrongs don't make a right"? On the flip side of this, there was public shaming online as a result of some of the super bloom pics that were posted to social media websites. One woman proudly displayed her bouquet of uprooted poppies, only to be torn apart online afterward. One person wrote, "Here's a new low. Not just trampling. Not just picking flowers. But pulling the entire plant, roots and all, out of the ground! … You can still see dirt dangling from the roots … this 'influencer' was there with children. What do you think those children learned? … Someone please make this stupidity stop."[6] Others, of course, joined in on the shaming, making a bad situation even worse.

I suspect you may be feeling a bit uneasy with all of this horrible and cruel behavior that is infiltrating our society. No worries, as I have faith that we can do something about it! Case in point, Mothers Against Drunk Drivers (MADD) is a grassroots movement that was started in 1980 by one mom. And throughout the years, MADD has changed the course of history in the U.S. and around the world.

"Racism and all the other 'isms' grow from primitive tribalism, the instinctive hostility against those of another tribe, race, religion, nationality, class or whatever."

— Roger Ebert

---

6 https://www.theguardian.com/environment/2019/apr/09/influencers-national-parks-public-lands-hate-you?sfns=mo

THE IMPACT OF BULLYING ON OUR YOUTH

A culture of shame and negativity may seem innocent, but it's not. We should not encourage online bullies to continue to torture people with their mean-spirited messages. As children take their cues from adults, often emulating their behavior, what will stop them from validating the bad behavior they see online? What will prevent them from mimicking a lack of decency or self-restraint?

It is now customary to see celebrities attack and derogate others on social media. Online behavior is one thing. However, it inspires the same type of negative thinking and emboldens appalling behavior in real life. Our children learn from the negative examples perpetrated by their role models as they are forming their moral concepts.

The rational part of a young person's brain is not fully developed until age 25. Therefore, you can imagine the damage and harm that influences their sense of normalcy and decency. The irony here is that some children, those raised with strong values and morals, can distinguish the bad behavior from good. They are the children who ask why celebrities and political leaders are allowed to misbehave.

Witnessing negative online behavior and trying to reconcile it in a young person's brain is one thing. What about how online communication is limited in the feedback it provides to our children and youth?

For example, when you are communicating online, you are unable to read body language and hear a person's tone of voice to know if you may have unintentionally offended them. Moreover, because social media is devoid of social cues that would mitigate the same behavior in real life, there are no real-life consequences or laws to refrain from acting poorly online. To make matters worse, aggressive and bullying behavior is condoned on social media. Therefore, when the bully gets likes and retweets, it validates their bad behavior and encourages them to continue to act the same.

If you think that bullying doesn't hurt people – or worse, children – think again! Bullying, or being mean to kids on the playground, is not "part of being a kid." It should not be a regular part of child development.

Ikea partnered with schools across the United Arab Emirates to study the impact of bullying. Students were asked to bully one plant and say mean things such as "you look rotten," or "are you even alive?" The other plant received compliments and praise from students with phrases such as "I like the way you are," and "you're making a difference in the world." Both plants were provided with the same amount of water and sunlight. The only difference was the audio messages that they received on a loop for 30 days. The results were astonishing! The plants that received negative messages withered and died, whereas the plants that received the compliments and praise remained healthy. If that can happen to plants in 30 days, can you imagine the impact it has on people? Or, worse, how about young people who are incredibly impressionable and vulnerable.

According to BullyingStatistics.org, a Yale University study found that "Bully victims are between 2 to 9 times more likely to consider suicide than non-victims."[7] Moreover, ABC News reported that "nearly 30 percent of students are either bullies or victims of bullying, and 160,000 kids stay home from school every day because of fear of bullying."[8]

Boston Children's Hospital reports that "In the US, suicide is the 2nd leading cause of death among children and adolescents ages 10-24 ... Nearly

---

7 http://www.bullyingstatistics.org/content/bullying-and-suicide.html
8 http://www.bullyingstatistics.org/content/bullying-and-suicide.html

one of every eight children between the ages 6 and 12 has suicidal thoughts."[9] If you think it won't happen to someone you know, think again. The hospital goes on to say, "suicide crosses all age, racial, and socioeconomic groups in the US and around the world."[10]

These are not just anonymous statistics. In August 2018, a nine-year-old Colorado boy killed himself after being bullied because he was gay.[11] In December 2018, a nine-year-old girl took her own life after being taunted by racist bullies at her Alabama school.[12] In April 2019, a Syrian nine-year-old committed suicide after being bullied by cruel classmates who called her ugly.[13]

Must I continue? These were kids who were tormented so viciously by other kids that they could take it no more and decided to end their lives. If this doesn't wake us up to the insanity, I honestly do not know what will. I trust, like me, you have a sick feeling in the pit of your stomach. It means that we have not yet become numb to it all. More importantly, it means that we CAN do something about it!

If reading about how bullying negatively affects children has you feeling sickened and also inspired to do something about it, feel free to skip past the tribalism section and get to the 'feel-good stuff' that I'm hoping induced you to read my chapter in the first place.

TOXIC TRIBALISM IS DESTROYING OUR

9 http://www.childrenshospital.org/conditions-and-treatments/conditions/s/suicide-and-teens/symptoms-and-causes

10 http://www.childrenshospital.org/conditions-and-treatments/conditions/s/suicide-and-teens/symptoms-and-causes

11 https://people.com/crime/colorado-boy-commits-suicide-after-school-bullying-being-gay/

12 https://nypost.com/2018/12/10/9-year-old-committed-suicide-after-classmates-taunted-kill-yourself-family/

13 https://globalnews.ca/news/5163138/calgary-syrian-family-daughter-suicide/

HUMANITY

Being a part of a community has been well-researched to have health benefits. Communities enable us to develop friendships and connect with others within our social circles. Communities enable us to meet new people and experience new cultures. Being a part of a community enables us to support each other and share our experiences and struggles. Communities provide resources for us to learn from each other and barter our skills and talents. But, more importantly, communities provide us with a profound sense of belonging and allow us to give back.

Healthy communities are great. However, communities can become toxic when they demand blind loyalty to one's tribe or social group, become dysfunctional, and when the dogma and negative behavior that results becomes normalized.

Toxic tribalism has a group mob mentality that sees the other group as bad or wrong, while they see their group as good or right. Tribalism discourages thinking for yourself or standing up for what you feel is right. You must surrender your integrity and honor at the door, or don't come in!

Common behaviors demonstrated with toxic tribalism include labeling the others with derogatory terms such as "evil," "racist," "scum," and "idiots." This tribal behavior becomes almost unconscious, as the person is unable to remain calm while having a conversation with someone from their own tribe who is playing devil's advocate, or refuses to listen to someone who is from the other tribe. People belong to these types of toxic tribes because it provides a sense of belonging.

However, unlike healthy communities, bad tribalism is built on a foundation of hate, disdain, anger, and jealousy. It demands primal blind allegiance.

Otherwise, you are considered a traitor.

Living with this type of judgment, anger, and rage is not healthy. There is a plethora of research demonstrating that stress over a long period suppresses an individual's immune system, which puts them at risk for infection, and worse, cancer. Moreover, anger can lead to a variety of health problems such as headaches, digestive issues, increased anxiety and depression, insomnia, high blood pressure, heart attacks, strokes, and skin problems such as eczema. If that doesn't scare you, "Having an episode of intense anger was associated with an 8.5 times greater risk of having a heart attack during the following two hours, a new study published in *The European Heart Journal Acute Cardiovascular Care* showed."[14]

Have you heard of the "Stanford Prison Experiment"? In August 1971, a team of researchers at Stanford University wanted to learn about the psychological effects on people who played the roles of a prisoner or prison officer. The study posed questions such as "What happens when you put good people in an evil place? Does humanity win over evil? Or, does evil triumph?" The study was supposed to last for two weeks but had to be stopped after only six days because of the behavior of the participants.

According to Professor Philip G. Zimbardo, the college students playing prison guards (correctional officers) became sadistic, and the students playing prisoners became depressed and displayed signs of extreme stress. The good prison officers felt helpless to intervene and were pressured to conform to the bad behavior. The impact of this study on regular college students demonstrates human nature and how kind and decent people can be influenced by others to misbehave.

Finally, we get to the good stuff! One of the founders of western philosophy,

---

14 http://time.com/3720718/anger-heart-attack/

Socrates, said, "The secret of change is to focus all of your energy, not on fighting the old, but on building the new."

BUT, IT DOESN'T HAVE TO BE THIS WAY!

In January 2000, President Bill Clinton delivered his State of the Union address to Congress. Clinton stated, "Modern science has confirmed what ancient faiths have always taught: the most important fact of life is our common humanity. Therefore, we should do more than just tolerate our diversity. We should honor it and celebrate it."[15]

Common humanity, honoring and celebrating diversity. Politics aside, I was so moved when I heard those words, that I couldn't help but notice a glimmer of hope being restored within me. My friend and I discussed the differences between healthy communities and toxic tribalism, which made me think about healthy tribalism.

I believe we can transition to a place where tribalism is decent, kind, and empathetic. A place where tribalism is generous and giving. A place where our human tribe, of which we ALL belong, can contribute to society in a positive way. A place where the only currency is to be honorable, respectful, and gracious. Ahhhh. That sounds so amazing. Don't you think?

WE CAN DO THIS! We can start by putting down our mobile devices and begin listening to each other. We can have an open heart and mind, and learn to accept each other with our differences. As we learn about people who come from different communities, countries, religions, and walks of life, we will naturally extend our hand to help each other. We will return to a state of decency, empathy, and grace. We will see that our common humanness is

15 https://www.nytimes.com/2000/01/28/us/state-union-president-clinton-state-union-strongest-it-has-ever-been.html

more important than any differences that we may have. English writer, poet, philologist, and academic, J.R.R. Tolkien said, "Even the smallest person can change the course of the future."

Our culture of selfishness and individualism can evolve into one of shared values. I believe that we were ALL created for a higher purpose. We have but one shot on earth to leave behind an imprint of who we are and what we stand for. What we say, and do not say, impacts others. It literally and figuratively changes the course of our existence. It affects our relationships, as it does the stranger passing you by on the street.

So, if you are frustrated with how poorly people are behaving around you – do something about it! We are allowed to change our minds at any time. While we may have condoned a behavior in the past, it doesn't mean that we must accept it always. Past the public façade of what image we want others to see, we get to decide who we indeed are.

We can make changes by beginning with a positive outlook. We can do an inventory of our strengths and weaknesses, and take responsibility for our transgressions. We can learn from our mistakes and focus on doing things better the next time. As bestselling author, poet, and activist, Maya Angelou says, "Do the best you can until you know better. Then when you know better, do better."

We all have old baggage that weighs us down and affects our relationships. But we don't have to allow it to normalize lousy behavior.

We can control our emotions with tools such as meditation and mindfulness. We can demonstrate grace and generosity. We can experience the joys and benefits of gratitude. We can work towards creating a kinder space for ourselves and future generations.

"The time is always right to do what is right."

— Martin Luther King, Jr.

WHEN YOU WITNESS BAD BEHAVIOR, MAKE A POSITIVE DIFFERENCE

Mahatma Gandhi, who led India to independence and inspired movements for civil rights and freedom across the world, said, "Be the change that you wish to see in the world." Well, Gandhi, I am going to heed your advice and be the change. I hope that I will inspire and encourage others to do the same.

What type of change do you want to see? When you witness or experience bad behavior first-hand, what can you do about it? Please try to keep these ideas in mind as you interact with others:

- **You never know what the other person is going through.** They could be leaving the hospital where their sick parent is dying. Or they may have just been dumped by their partner. We never know why people behave the way they do sometimes. So, instead of adding fuel to the flame, be the bigger person and offer some humility and grace.

- **Instead of responding with anger or judgment, respond with love** – even though it is sometimes hard. Feel empathy and compassion for the other person's predicament and refrain from becoming reactionary. Live at peace with everyone and be gentle.

- **We have more in common than we do that differs.** Share common ground, try to accept and respect differences, and discuss them openly and calmly.

- **Claim some ownership of the problem and address the other person's feelings.** Speak in "I" statements, such as "I understand you are upset." Sometimes individuals will calm down just knowing that they are being validated. It will also establish, or re-establish, some trust between you.

- **When the storm calms down, afterward reflect on why certain behaviors upset you** by isolating events/actions that triggered it. We all have different definitions of what qualifies as 'bad' behavior. You may be reacting to something that others would not because of your past (aka baggage). Doing this type of inventory will help prepare you for the next potential conflict.

- **Treat others as you would have them treat you.**

What ideas and actions can you implement to cause a change in your daily interactions and connections with others? How can you be the bigger person in the equation?

Are you ready to make a substantive change in your life? According to Virginia Tech University, the following are the "Stages of Change"[16]:

1. Precontemplation (not yet acknowledging that there is a problem behavior that needs to be changed)

2. Contemplation (acknowledging that there is a problem behavior but not yet ready or sure of wanting to make a change)

3. Preparation/Determination (getting ready to change)

4. Action/Willpower (changing behavior)

5. Maintenance (maintaining the behavior change)

6. Relapse (returning to older behaviors and abandoning the new changes)

BE AN EVERYDAY HERO

---

16 http://www.cpe.vt.edu/gttc/presentations/8eStagesofChange.pdf

Maya Angelou says, "I think a hero is any person really intent on making this a better place for all people."

What does a hero look like to you? To me, being a hero is:

- About rising to the occasion and being the best you can be

- A calling we all have and a desire to live with purpose and conviction

- Helping and serving others, and inspiring others to do the same

- Being a leader and a positive role model in your community

- Living within your moral values

- Being courageous, as it is not always easy to resolve conflict or stand up to bullies

- Calling out people when you see them misbehave

- Being a good child, sibling, parent, spouse, friend, neighbor, or colleague

- Being respectful to your teachers and elders

- Emulating other heroes in your life

- Demonstrating integrity, humility, and a desire to change

I recently saw a video on YouTube that helped to restore my faith in humanity. In the wake of the terrorist attacks in Manchester, London, a Muslim man, Baktash Noori, offered free hugs to people. In his effort to demonstrate unity and combat Islamophobia, he wore a blindfold and stood next to a sign that read "I'm Muslim and I trust you. Do you trust me enough for a hug?" In this real-life social experiment, dozens of people lined up to hug Noori.[17] If a young Muslim man can allow himself to be vulnerable in a city recovering from the aftermath of a brutal terror attack, we can too!

---

17 https://www.youtube.com/watch?v=XS_tACfzfaI

Part of being the change is inspiring others to do the same. Jim Rohn, the world-renowned motivational speaker and philosopher said, "You are the average of the five people you spend the most time with."

Who are the five people you spend the most time with? When was the last time you looked at your friends and evaluated your 'friendships' to see if they are still working for you? How do you know if your friends are a good, or bad, influence on you? Worse, are your friends harming your health?

HOW TO KNOW IF YOU ARE FRIENDS WITH A WRETCH ... (OR SUBSTITUTE YOUR OWN ADJECTIVE!)

Take a moment to complete this fun quiz:
(For the sake of clarity, we will call your 'bad' friend "Frollo.")

1. **Your mother calls you to find out how your weekend went. After telling her that you spent time with your friend Frollo, she responds:**

   a. That's nice. What did you do?

   b. Did you say Frollo? Didn't you have anything better to do?

   c. You did what? I thought I told you that Frollo was terrible for you!

2. **After getting a promotion at work, you are excited to share the great news with your friend Frollo, who responds:**

   a. Wow, I'm so happy for you. Let's celebrate!

   b. You're lucky I don't work there or that promotion would have been mine.

   c. Why are you making such a big deal about it? You are so arrogant!

3. **You are feeling great about losing 25 pounds and fitting into your summer clothes again. You put a lot of hard work into it by eating healthy and working out four times a week. After sharing the news with your friend, Frollo responds:**

   a. You worked so hard. I'm so proud of you!

   b. I can't tell. It must be water weight.

   c. You know you are going to sabotage yourself and gain it all back again!

4. **You are studying for your exams, and have spent every waking hour working towards keeping your 4.0 GPA when Frollo calls with a 'favor' to ask. You try to say no and explain why you can't afford to lose six hours of study time. Frollo responds:**

   a. I completely understand. I know how important your GPA is to you. Don't worry, I will figure something out.

   b. That sucks. I do a lot of things for you. I wish you would repay the favor.

   c. I can't believe how selfish you are. I'm supposed to be your best friend. Is this how best friends treat each other? You may as well leave me stranded on the side of the road without any money or a cellular phone!

5. **You get home after spending a long day with Frollo, and you feel:**

   a. Energized and excited about what a great time you had with your best friend. You are so grateful to have someone as special as Frollo in your life.

   b. A bit bummed that you wasted so much time driving Frollo all over town when you had a lot of important stuff to do.

c. Stressed out and upset that Frollo was so insensitive and mean towards you. You can't help but question your friendship.

Frollo Friendship Quiz Results:

- **If you scored mostly A's**, then congratulations! You have a healthy, supportive friendship that you should hold on to and cherish.

- **If you scored mostly B's**, then you may need to pull back from the 'friendship' and spend time with people who make you feel better about yourself.

- **If you scored mostly C's**, then do yourself a favor and run for the hills! Seriously, it's time to cut the cord and end the friendship. It is best to be honest and say that the friendship is no longer working for you, and wish Frollo well. Name-calling and finger-pointing will not solve anything, and you will probably lose an argument with a person whose inherent nature is to be cruel.

"Things do not change; we change."

— Henry David Thoreau

In closing, I want to thank you for spending your valuable time reading my chapter.

I believe that unless we work towards being our best selves, or at least better versions of ourselves than we were yesterday, we will need to learn how to deal with profound disappointment in humanity.

Theo Spanos Dunfey, Executive Director of Global Citizens Circle, writes, "Well known examples of such change have resulted from social movements in civil rights, women's rights, … Relationships have changed, institutions have changed, and cultural norms have changed as a result of these social change movements."

Everyday people like you and me started these movements. I have hope, as there are social movements and positive changes going on all around us:

- Western medical practitioners now understand the benefits of meditation

- There has been groundbreaking research in the area of positive psychology

- There is a gratitude movement that has people feeling better about themselves

- People are joining positive, supportive communities that help them to learn and grow

- Diversity is all around us and it's represented in mainstream media and advertising

Yes, I do believe positive change is happening! Can you think of any other examples of positive change? If so, hang on to them, as they will help to carry us through some tough, and potentially dark, days ahead.

Finally, I leave you with an inspirational quote from Nelson Mandela, the father of the modern nation of South Africa, whose wisdom resonates with millions of people around the world and whose legend will endure for many, many years to come.

"I learned that courage was not the absence of fear, but the triumph over it. The brave man is not he who does not feel afraid, but he who conquers that fear."

— Nelson Mandela

The Pathway to Achieve Your Dream Life!

PHIL ARMSTRONG

This chapter will begin to illuminate your world in a way that will make lasting change possible. I want for you whatever big dreams you have, and I can certainly put you on the path to achieving them. But I also have a word of caution for you as you dream these big dreams: at some point you're going to begin to hear an inner voice say, "You can't do that!" Well, I say to you ignore that voice, because he is a liar. He represents a part of you that wants comfort not change, relaxation not tireless pursuit, and certainty instead of self-confidence. This is your worst enemy.

So, first and foremost, you must identify and get passed the liar in your head. To do this, you'll have to learn to listen for the voice and then practice not taking its advice. Also, learn to distinguish between the negative and the positive voices in your head (yes, there's more than one voice!). It may seem difficult at first, but I have every reason to believe whatever your mind can conceive—along with Desire, Faith, Focus, Determination, and Action—your mind can achieve.

DESIRE

Desire is the starting point of all achievement. To create or cultivate desire, you must know what it is you want from life—the type of lifestyle, the kind of relationships, even the amount of money you want to earn and keep. Specifically, you need to sit down with paper and pen and define the things you want. Once you have created both a physical and a mental picture of them, then you can think about setting some goals to achieve them.

So, let me get you started. Take time now to answer the questions below. They're meant to help you get a better glimpse of your purpose and create some desire to take action.

1. What makes you smile?

2. What are your favorite things to do?

3. What activities make you lose track of time?

4. What makes you feel great about yourself?

5. Who inspires you most?

6. What are you naturally good at?

7. What do others ask for your help with?

8. If you had to teach, what would you teach?

Note: for a complete list pick up my book, "The Keys to Think and Grow Rich," set up a coaching session or ask about one of my seminars in your area. I can be reached at armstrongbreakthrough.com.

In addition to the desire to take action, you really do need to put good thoughts into your head instead of lousy ones. Why? Because you need to be in a good place to conquer the list of the top reasons people fail. Some of these include:

1. Lack of well-defined purpose in life

2. Lack of ambition to aim above mediocrity

3. Insufficient education

4. Lack of self-discipline

5. Ill health

6. Procrastination

7. Lack of persistence

8. Negative personality

As you go over this list, study yourself to discover how many of these causes of failure stand between you and success.

For a full list pick up my book, set up a coaching session, or ask about one of my seminars in your area. Go to armstrongbreakthrough.com.

Next, I want you to ask yourself this question: are you just interested in achieving your dreams and desires, or are you committed to achieving them?

Those who are just interested will do what's easy, and what everybody else does, while the committed ones will do what it takes—they'll practice, study and put in the effort to persevere until their desires are achieved. They won't make excuses, they'll stop blaming and they'll give up their victim stories. Instead, they'll focus on how they can achieve their goals.

The way to achieve your goals is to:

1. Fix in your mind exactly what it is that you desire. Write it down.

2. Determine exactly what you intend to give in return for what you want. Write it down.

3. Establish a definite date when you intend to acquire what you want. Write it down.

4. Create a definite plan for carrying out your desire. Write it down.

5. Begin to put your plan into action, whether you're ready or not.

6. For each goal you're working on, read your written statements out loud, twice-daily—once just before retiring at night and once after rising in the morning.

Note: repeat the process for each specific goal you have (by writing out a clear, concise statement of the goal you intend to achieve, naming the time limit for its achievement, stating what you intend to give in return for it and describing clearly the plan through which you intend to achieve it).

As you read, see and believe yourself already in possession of what it is that you want.

In my book, "The Keys to Think and Grow Rich," I talk about the Four Pillars of Goal Setting: Financial, Health & Fitness, Relationships & Spiritual, and Legacy & Charity. Pick up a copy, set up a coaching session, or enquire about our seminar package. You can do this at armstrongbreakthrough.com.

FAITH

Is all it takes to achieve your dreams desire and a bunch of well-defined goals? Not a chance. You'll need faith.

Faith is a state of mind—an active state of mind—in which the mind is in the process of relating itself to the great vital force of the universe. The best way faith can be explained is to say that it's—humanity's awareness of, belief in and harmonizing with the universal power surrounding him. Faith establishes a working association with the power variously referred to as the Universal Mind, the Divine Mind, and by religionists, as God.

Faith may be induced, or accessed, by affirmation or repeated instructions to the Subconscious Mind through the principle of auto-suggestion. Repetition of orders given to your Subconscious Mind is the only known method of voluntary development of the emotion of faith. All thoughts that have been emotionalized (given feeling), and mixed wth faith, begin immediately to translatc thcmsclvcs into thcir physical cquivalent or counterpart. The emotions, or the feeling portion of thoughts, are the factors that give faith, vitality, life and action.

Please note that the Subconscious Mind does not discriminate between constructive thoughts or negative thoughts, and will work with the material we feed it. Through our thought impulses, the Subconscious Mind will translate into reality a thought driven by fear just as readily as it will translate into reality as a thought driven by courage or faith.

Your belief, or your faith, is the element that determines the action of your Subconscious Mind.

There's nothing to hinder you from deceiving your Subconscious Mind when giving it instructions through auto-suggestion. To make this deceit more realistic, conduct yourself as you would if you were already in possession of what you're suggesting to your mind. One believes whatever one repeats to oneself. Every man is what he is because of the dominating thoughts that he permits to occupy his mind. Repeat a lie enough times and you will begin to believe it is true.

To help you get a better understanding of how the mind works to bring into your life the people, the places and the things that you need to build your dreams, consider the following stories.

THE PLACEBO EFFECT

A recent Baylor College of Medicine study on the outcome of arthroscopic knee surgery demonstrates the placebo effect. A group of patients with painful and worn-out knee joints were given two types of surgery: one group had the actual surgery, and the other was just given a surgical scar. Two years later, patients reported equal improvement in pain relief and knee function. There are thousands of studies such as this, showing the placebo medication or surgery was as effective as the real thing. Why? The Subconscious Mind was told that it would work, and it expected to do just that! Remember, the Subconscious Mind cannot tell the difference between the real and the imaginary.

TUG MCGRAW— YOU GOTTA BELIEVE!

Few people know that when Phillies pitcher Tug McGraw struck out batter Willie Wilson, in the bottom of the ninth to win the 1980 World Series, the game played out exactly as Tug planned it. When interviewed and asked how he felt at that tense moment, Tug surprised them when he said, "It was as if I'd been there a thousand times before. When I was growing up, I would pitch to my father in the backyard. It would always get to the place where it was the bottom of the ninth, three men on, and two outs. I would bear down and strike out that last man to win the World Series." Because Tug conditioned his mind, day after day, in the backyard, the day eventually arrived where he was living out that dream for real.

The previous story reminds me to tell you a little about The Law of Attraction. When I think of faith I often use this law. It states that if you put yourself out into the universe, then whatever it is you desire will begin to move toward you. The stronger your faith, the stronger the attraction. Learn more about this law by picking up my book, "The Keys to Think and Grow Rich," setting up a coaching session, or asking about one of my seminars in your area. I can be reached at armstrongbreakthrough.com.

FOCUS

What can I say about the power of adding focus to your life? People like Earl Nightingale, Maxwell Maltz and Napoleon Hill became famous for their discoveries of the importance of focusing your thoughts on the positive; on those things you want in your life. Conversely, they understood the opposite was also true: you must guard against thoughts other than those you want in your life. In fact, they had in their hands the very cure to the ills of this world—looking to the light rather than to the dark, zooming in on the positive rather than entertaining the negative, saying yes to life rather than saying no.

But if it really is that simple, then why isn't everyone healthy, wealthy and happy? It goes back to my earlier comments regarding the way the Subconscious Mind works. The subconscious can't tell real from imagined, and it has no filter other than the choices you make; the thoughts you choose to focus on are what it has to work with. You can make this process easier by internalizing these thoughts with strong emotion, dialing up the focus, so to speak. It's here where most people get in trouble.

Nobody in school ever taught you that your Subconscious Mind is what will bring the world to your doorstep. No one ever told you to ay attention to the conversation in your head, because your subconscious is listening too. The average person thinks tens of thousands of thoughts every day and is only aware of a small fraction of them. Of those thoughts they are aware of, very few are placed there "on purpose" and with forethought as to what they want those thoughts to do. Finally, average people definitely don't know how to best focus those thoughts for winning results.

Affirmations, written or oral statements that confirm something is true, are the missing key. The person who stands before the mirror and says with conviction, "I will earn an extra thousand this month." may feel silly, especially when he or she says it ten times in a row morning and night. But that person (you) is focusing those thoughts. When you use affirmations, you are painting a bullseye on your Subconscious Mind (or Spirit). Remember, the subconscious can't tell real from imagined. It will, instead, get to work on making that affirmation happen for you.

Furthermore, thoughts you continuously impress upon your Subconscious Mind over and over become fixed in that part your personality. Fixed ideas will then continue to express themselves without any conscious assistance until they are replaced, something we refer to as a habit.

All this may sound a bit out there, but it has been proven to work. The body is the material presentation of you. It's an instrument of the mind. Your thoughts are impressed upon the Subconscious Mind which moves your body into action, which produces your results. Your Conscious Mind thinks, your Subconscious Mind feels and your Body produces action, which determines your results.

$$\text{Thought} + \text{Emotion} = \text{Action}$$

DETERMINATION

Determination when pursuing big dreams is all about being resolved to do the things you must do in order to achieve those dreams. It's about replacing thoughts of doubt with positive thoughts that elicit useful emotions, especially when facing obstacles that appear to be insurmountable.

Again, we come back to the two mind theory: the Conscious Mind, which reasons, and the Subconscious Mind, which feels. Put the two of them together, working in unison, and you get strong action as a result.

But let's consider this in reverse. What's happening when emotions bubble up from the subconscious unsummoned (these could be positive or negative in nature)? A habit has been triggered. A habit you may not even be aware exists. A habit that can, and will, threaten your determination to carry out your action steps or goals. How? If the triggered emotion is strong enough and the action it tends to bring about is one you resort to a lot, then you could find yourself taking actions completely opposite to the ones you need to be taking.

Such habits have probably been created without you ever being aware of what was happening. This is why it's important to pay attention (at least in situations involving your dreams and goals) to your self-talk. You see, the thoughts—and the emotions they evoke—are the result of your two minds communicating with each other, and they can give you a pretty clear picture of what's going on.

So, if you discover that your self-talk isn't helping you at the moment, I want you to remember that you have the freedom of choice to change it (by using affirmations). Don't make the mistake of thinking that you are locked into a certain way of thinking or feeling. It simply takes a little longer to communicate with your Subconscious or Spirit Mind than it does with your Conscious Mind. Let me give you an example.

Penny is feeling dejected this morning. She can't seem to get motivated. There's a presentation on her desk for a client she's meeting at 1 p.m. and all Penny can think about is going for a walk in the park. She remembers a seminar she went to that taught people how to change their thoughts and emotions into more useful ones. Penny writes some sentences on a piece of paper, and then grabs her purse and heads to the washroom.

Standing in front of the washroom mirror, Penny recites what she has written down, 10 times for each sentence.

- Winston (her client) trusts me.

- This solution will work for him.

- The sale is guaranteed!

Penny then rubs her hands together quickly for a few seconds before clapping them together and saying "Yes!" in an excited voice. A thrill of emotion runs through her and she's suddenly energized (like she was in the seminar where she learned to do this). Her thoughts immediately turn to her presentation, so she returns to her desk and goes back to work.

To learn more please contact me at armstrongbreakthrough.com.

ACTION

As you can see, getting results is all about motivating yourself (specifically your body) to take pre-planned actions specifically designed to produce said results. Notice I said "pre-planned actions." Motivation for those actions depends on how the Conscious and Subconscious Minds interact. So, writing down your goals forces you to think those exact words. Doing affirmations further instructs the mind and brings emotion and your subconscious into play, which is where your motivation to act will come from. Usually, the greater the emotion, the greater the motivation to act.

People will look at you funny if you tell them you are pre-planning your actions for tomorrow, but I find it strange that anyone would choose any other way of going through life than "on purpose." Think about it. Most people go through their days buffeted by the winds of life. They don't live "on purpose," and that's a shame. We have free will for a reason. You get to choose what you do and what things mean to you every single second of every day.

Think about that for a few minutes! You can actually decide what anything means. A death can be a blessing. Or it can be sad. It can also be a reason to celebrate the person's life. Your past, something the average person drags along into the future with them, doesn't have to have any meaning at all. It's just a bunch of things that happened to you. You are free to just BE IN THE

MOMENT, open to all the possibilities of the future and ready to spring into action with your dreams and goals firmly in mind. There's another way of saying all this …

Every January over 65 % of Americans make new year's resolutions, and 92 % of these people never achieve them. A Harvard MBA study showed that 3 % had written goals and plans, and 13 % had goals but only in their mind, while the remaining 84 % had no goals. 10 years later it was found that the 13 % earned twice as much as the 84 % and the 3 % earned 10 times as much as the 97 percent combined.

In his best seller book, "Think and Grow Rich," Napoleon Hill states that setting goals and plans to achieve them is the starting point of all achievement. I can't think of a better reason for being "on purpose" in this life.

One little reminder: when you take pre-planned action, make sure it covers every base and then some. In other words, take MASSIVE ACTION!

Want to learn more? Send me an email at armstrongbreakthrough.com

THE UNIVERSAL ALL

The Universal All is something I came up with to discuss the one aspect of achievement that we haven't yet visited. There are thousands of other names for this power but rather than just define the name, I want to define the activity. You see, for three thousand years all the great thinkers have all agreed upon one point—that there is a power, and this power creates, animates and motivates the entire cosmos.

How does this power animate and motivate? What are some of its distinguishing features? To determine the answer to my question we will first refer to the school of science and the school of theology.

> Science, the study of knowledge, calls it "Energy."
> What is energy? They say it just is!
> It's neither created nor destroyed.
> It's the cause and effect of itself.
> It's 100% present in all places at all times.

> What does theology say this power is?
> They say it is "God."
> Describe God. He just is.
> He's neither created nor destroyed.
> He's the cause and effect of himself.
> He's 100% in all places at all times.

Wernher von Braun, father of the space program, stated that "science studies this force that surrounds humanity and theology studies this force that is within humanity. Someday they will agree that they are studying the same thing."

I believe that to gain the good life we all desire so much, we must understand how to relate to this great power. We don't necessarily have to understand it— that's the faith part of things— but we do need to know that we're part of it. Just remember, theology studies the spirit, while science studies the physical.

When we say we are burned out, we are referring to both energy (the physical) and emotions (the spiritual). When we say we are motivated, we are also saying we are energized. When we act, we can feel both the physical and the emotional components of that state.

So, if I can use my conscious mind, which is more a part of the physical world, to energize my subconscious or spirit mind, then it begs the question—are these things not related? Is it possible that they may even be the same thing? And if they are, how can we use this knowledge?

In real life, there appears to be a veil between the physical and the spiritual. As we attempt to communicate across that veil it seems that we need to purposefully place our communications into the physical or conscious mind. We can do this best by sight. We write things down and look at them, placing them firmly into our mind as bold thoughts. Then we must purposefully place our communications into the Spirit or Subconscious Mind. We do this vocally and with emotions. We feel what we want as we say what we want. The result is some level of action being asked of our bodies. We're summoned. The higher the energy and the higher the emotion we achieve, the greater the action of which we are capable becomes. Interesting stuff.

SUMMARY

Whatever your mind can conceive of your mind can also achieve. This is a fundamental truth, but there is a part of you that I refer to as the liar. Its voice will appear in your head as you progress through ever more challenging goals. This part of you wants comfort not change, relaxation not tireless pursuit, and certainty instead of self-confidence. Luckily, you also have a positive voice—a helper—that will allow you to counter the effects of the liar's voice on your psyche. Unless you have a very good reason to do otherwise, listen to your helper and ignore the liar. Once passed the liar, achievement is a matter of following a prescribed set of steps. These include: desire, faith, focus, determination, and action.

DESIRE: It's easier to dream big, and to create both a mental and written picture of these things, if you create a list of things you love to do that will solve problems for the people who surround you. It's better than the alternative of continuing to follow rules that just don't work. Think about this as you progress from dreams to concrete goals and action steps. We also reviewed a partial list of common causes of failure.

The way to achieve your goals is to write out a clear, concise statement of each goal you intend to attain, name the time limit for its attainment, state what you intend to give in return for it and describe clearly the plan through which you intend to achieve it. Read your written statements out loud, twice-daily: once just before retiring at night and once after rising in the morning.

FAITH: Your mind is driven by thoughts; your body is driven by emotion. Faith is an emotion. It's something that happens when we try to connect to the universe around us. Wrap specific thoughts or calls to action in the emotion of faith—through written and spoken affirmations—and your Subconscious Mind will go to work on the problem. This will usually put your body to work on the problem (motivation). Note: the Subconscious Mind can't tell the difference a between real or imagined experience. This means you can manipulate it to do your bidding.

FOCUS: Thought + Emotion = Action. You can extrapolate that if certain thoughts and emotions are focused on the Subconscious Mind, then your motivation will be dialed up as well. This happens to be true. You just have to make your affirmations as convincing as possible. Also, the more you repeat your affirmations, the greater and more focused the actions you are eliciting become, until what you've been after becomes a habit you don't have to think about anymore.

DETERMINATION: It's all about being resolved to do a thing, to choose to bring to bear both the Conscious Mind (reason and thought) and the

Subconscious Mind (emotions), until you are motivated to take massive action with respect to solving one of your goals. The tool you use for this is affirmations.

ACTION: You can decide how you're going to act in advance by using affirmation to create a habit. One thing that arises from this truth is that you don't have to act in certain ways in a given situation. The corollary is that you decide what things mean. Decide what things mean to you—in any given moment—and it results in personal freedom; the freedom to be in the moment, to do anything, to BE anything, to choose from all the possibilities of the future that lies before you.

THE UNIVERSAL ALL: For three thousand years all the great thinkers have all agreed upon one point—that there is a power, and this power creates, animates and motivates the entire cosmos, including you. Scientists call it Energy, religionists call it God. What you call it may not matter because IT is in you. The subconscious represents the physical and the subconscious represents the emotional. What if they are the same thing in different forms?

www.ingramcontent.com/pod-product-compliance
Lightning Source LLC
Chambersburg PA
CBHW070349090426
42733CB00009B/1345